THE BATTLE OF
FIRST DEEP BOTTOM

THE BATTLE OF
FIRST DEEP BOTTOM

JAMES S. PRICE

THE
History
PRESS

Published by The History Press
Charleston, SC 29403
www.historypress.net

Cover image: William Waud, "General Grant's Campaign—Capture of Four Twenty-Pound
Parrot Guns by Miles's Brigade, Barlow's Division, July 27, 1864," *Harper's Weekly*.

First published 2014

ISBN 978-1-5402-0680-0

Library of Congress CIP data applied for

CONTENTS

FOREWORD

On June 20, 1864, Brigadier General Godfrey Weitzel, a young Union engineer, tramped along the south bank of the James River across from Deep Bottom, an area at the apex of a hairpin curve in the river's course. Looking for an ideal location to place a pontoon bridge, Weitzel identified the best spot he could find. Within hours, a bridge spanned the James and Union troops had secured a lodgment on the north bank, only a few miles east of Richmond. Within weeks, substantial works covered the position, manned by a full brigade. With this operation, Ulysses S. Grant had established a bridgehead at Deep Bottom, an achievement that would help shape the balance of the Richmond-Petersburg Campaign, one of the war's most complex, lengthy and overlooked periods of military struggle.

It was not until late July, during his third offensive of the long campaign, that Grant would seek benefits from the Deep Bottom position by sending the II Corps, along with two divisions of cavalry, across the James to threaten Rebel positions there. The resulting engagements would become known as the First Battle of Deep Bottom. With many of Robert E. Lee's men dispatched to meet the threat there on the north side of the James, the Federals set their sights on Petersburg, detonating a mine under the Confederate lines east of the city and triggering the bloody, fruitless Crater battle.

In many historical accounts, the Deep Bottom operation appears in the limited role as the precursor of the Crater fight. To be sure, Union operations at Deep Bottom served to divert Confederate forces from Petersburg and enhance the possibility of the mine's success. However, the Deep Bottom fighting bears additional significance, for it provides a window into the rest of the overall campaign. For the first time, Grant and his commanders conducted extensive operations outside Richmond in an effort to distract the Confederates and gain ground to the south at Petersburg. In doing so, he ordered his commanders to hit the Confederates in two widely separated locations. Grant would use this basic recipe, with uneven success, repeatedly throughout the campaign. Over a series of six subsequent offensives, he would attack the Confederate positions. In each operation, he would vary the timing, weight and emphasis of the twin attacking columns. However, in nearly every instance, he would consistently threaten the Confederate defenses in one place to hamper Confederate efforts to concentrate forces elsewhere. This string of operations illustrated Grant's persistence, flexibility and willingness to try different approaches. However, he would not achieve total success until the ninth and final offensive in April 1865, when Petersburg fell and troops under Godfrey Weitzel's command marched into Richmond.

For Robert E. Lee, the Deep Bottom fighting in July presaged the challenges that he would face defending Richmond. Back in June, he had immediately recognized the threat posed by the Deep Bottom bridgehead, but with his forces overwhelmed at Petersburg, he could not conjure an effective response. As Grant picked and chose where to assault over the ensuing months, Lee scrambled to defend many miles of front divided by two rivers. He could not deploy his men in force everywhere. But when the Union probes appeared at Deep Bottom in July, he acted quickly to reinforce that sector and avoid disaster.

The First Battle of Deep Bottom also highlighted the struggles of the sorely overused Union II Corps, led by Winfield Hancock. This formation had served as the Army of the Potomac's shock troops throughout the fighting in 1864, carrying a heavy load in the Wilderness, at Spotsylvania and at Cold Harbor. By June, it had lost thousands to wounds and worse.

During the initial assaults against Petersburg, some II Corps units simply refused orders to attack. One week later, on June 22, the command crumpled under a Confederate assault along the Jerusalem Plank Road. As summer arrived in Petersburg, the formation was unraveling and so was the health of its commander. Suffering from a wound received at Gettysburg the year before, Winfield Hancock was much impaired. However, for him, First Deep Bottom stood out as a rare chance for independent command, along with the risks and opportunities it entailed.

Jimmy Price has done a great service by bringing the First Battle of Deep Bottom to light with this volume. On the heels of his insightful work chronicling the Union capture of New Market Heights in September 1864, this new study combines diligent research and clear writing into a concise, informative narrative. Harnessing his skills as a historian, battlefield guide and preservationist, Price examines these engagements in their own right and not as simply an appendage to the Crater battle. At the same time, he attends to the broader picture, framing the fighting in the context of the overall Richmond-Petersburg Campaign. The resulting work contributes greatly to the understanding of this important yet often overlooked aspect of the military operations during the war's last year.

Hampton Newsome
Arlington, Virginia
July 22, 2014

Preface

"WHO WILL WRITE UP THE DEEP BOTTOM FIGHTS?"

Nearly two decades had passed since the battle that took a chunk of old Ben Naylor's chin, and his patience for recognition was wearing thin. For nineteen years, reams of paper and incalculable gallons of ink had been spilled detailing the greatest battles of America's Civil War. The Gettysburg Battlefield was fast on its way to becoming the "world's largest outdoor sculpture garden," filled with monuments and heroic statues memorializing those three unforgettable days in 1863—yet no one had taken up the pen or given much thought at all to another three-day affair that, for poor Naylor, inflicted a wound that "stopped me from eating hard-tack and salt horse for a few days."

Naylor was one of many Union veterans who perused the section of the *National Tribune* newspaper styled "Fighting Them Over: What Our Veterans Have to Say about Their Old Campaigns," and every time he read this section, he searched in vain for more details about the clash of arms that had partially disfigured him. At some point, he grew frustrated enough to take matters into his own hands, and his letter to the editor of the *Tribune* was triumphantly published on October 18, 1883.

In it, he pleaded with his surviving comrades, "If this request should be seen by any of the boys of the 1st Brigade, 1st Division 2nd Army Corps who are handy with the pen, will they not give a few lines about Deep Bottom, where three regiments of our brigade captured four 24-pounders?" After all, the capture of four state-of-the-art cannons (though they were actually twenty-pounders) was nothing to sneeze at, especially when those guns were manned by artillerists fighting under Robert E. Lee.

Developing his tale to the *Tribune*'s readers, Naylor then expounded on his question and made sure that his chin would be enshrined in the annals of the rebellion for all time:

> *I was not in at the death, but I have a recollection of marching across an open field while the "blasted" shells were tearing up the ground, and then starting up the hill, when the infantry opened on us, and one of those little fellows that make such a "sickening thud" when a fellow happens to be in the way scraped the bark off my chin.*

The letter was signed "B.F. Naylor, Co. D, 183rd Pa. V.I., San Juan, CA." The question put forward as its title still stands to this very day: "Who Will Write Up the Deep Bottom Fights?"

The First Battle of Deep Bottom—also on occasion referred to as the Battle of Darbytown, Strawberry Plains, Tilghman's Gate, New Market Road, Gravel Hill and even Malvern Hill (the latter causing a great deal of confusion)—has been relegated to the status of a historical footnote. Part of Grant's Third Offensive of the Richmond-Petersburg Campaign, First Deep Bottom has been overshadowed by the more famous half of this operation: the epic catastrophe we now know as the Battle of the Crater. One would think that an expedition to threaten the Confederate capital led by such Union luminaries as Winfield Scott Hancock and Philip H. Sheridan would have garnered a substantial amount of attention by Civil War scholars, but this has not been the case.

So, what exactly took place during this first scuffle at Deep Bottom, and does it hold any lasting interest and value for those of us whose chins remain unscathed?

The first clash at Deep Bottom resulted from an expedition to the north side of the James River that was to coincide with Ambrose Burnside's mine assault at Petersburg. Hancock's II Corps, along with two divisions of Sheridan's cavalry and Major General August V. Kautz's Army of the James cavalry division, would cross the James River at Deep Bottom and threaten Richmond. The cavalry was to ride hard and fast to destroy the Virginia Central Railroad as far as the South Anna River. The blue cavaliers were then to ride down to Richmond and attempt to carry the city in a joint effort with the II Corps. If the raid was successful in destroying the railroad and taking Richmond, Grant intended to call off the mine attack. That was the plan, in theory—in practice, the expedition was a fiasco that was beset with problems before the first shots were fired.

Bryce A. Suderow, the leading authority on the battle, has attempted over the past two decades to answer the question he formally posed in 2000: "How was it that…three paragons of Union aggressiveness [Grant, Hancock and Sheridan] mismanaged a marvelous opportunity to defeat a portion of Lee's army and march into Richmond?" Regrettably, Suderow has been one of the few historians who have continued to pursue an answer. Until the publication of this study, the First Battle of Deep Bottom has only been the subject of footnotes, articles and book chapters. What remains to this day the definitive account of the battle is Suderow's own "Glory Denied: The First Battle of Deep Bottom, July 27th–29th, 1864," which first appeared in *North & South* magazine in September 2000. Four years later saw the publication of Dr. Louis H. Manarin's massive two-volume *Henrico County: Field of Honor*, which devoted a chapter to Hancock's first expedition north of the James River. Most recently, John F. Schmutz and Earl J. Hess have devoted chapters to First Deep Bottom in their respective books about the Battle of the Crater.

Thus, while the groundwork for an overall history of the First Battle of Deep Bottom has been laid, a general synthesis of these disparate sources into one cohesive narrative is necessary as the sesquicentennial commemoration of the American Civil War continues. It is my hope that this book will be the starting point for all who wish to further their understanding of this important action and the tone that it would set for the confrontations between Grant and Lee for the remainder of 1864.

As is the case with any historical work, the list of people to whom I owe thanks would take up half of the following pages if I were to name them all. However, a few individuals must be named for helping to bring this project to fruition.

The first person to whom the largest debt of gratitude must go is Bryce Suderow, who is the unparalleled expert on all things pertaining to First Deep Bottom. Bryce has been working on the definitive history of the battle for many years now, yet he was more than willing to help me with this project through phone conversations and e-mail. He also sent me a wealth of source material that he had compiled over the years, and I think it is safe to say that this project simply would not have happened were it not for his generosity.

Banks Smither, my commissioning editor at The History Press, was also of great help in bringing this book to fruition. I consider it a high honor that I now have two books with The History Press that will stand alongside the other excellent titles in its Civil War Sesquicentennial Series.

Hampton Newsome, himself an author of two excellent Civil War titles, took the time out of his busy schedule to read early portions of the manuscript and write a foreword.

Don Caughey, who writes the excellent blog "Regular Cavalry in the Civil War," did the original research on Medal of Honor recipient Timothy O'Connor of the 1st U.S. Cavalry, whose complete story is told for the first time in this book.

Master cartographer Steven Stanley was kind enough to work with me a second time, providing exceptional maps detailing the fighting on July 27 and 28, 1864.

Last but not least, I would like to thank my lovely wife, Gina, for her tender love and support.

Soli deo gloria.

Chapter 1

THE PROGRESS OF OUR ARMS

"CHEW AND CHOKE AS MUCH AS POSSIBLE"

It had been a summer drenched in blood.

While the trees and flowers were in vernal bloom, the expectations of thousands had also blossomed afresh in the hopes that the coming campaign season of 1864 would hammer the final nail in the coffin of the rebellion. As spring turned to summer, these hopes were dashed as the numbers of dead and maimed escalated with no clear end in sight.

On March 12, 1864, freshly minted Lieutenant General Ulysses S. Grant was given supreme command of the armies of the United States. Grant came from the Western Theater of operations, where he had seen wild success at places like Vicksburg and Chattanooga. He came east, where the Union cause had not fared so well, and quickly put into motion a plan that called for a concerted drive that spanned the entire chessboard of war. Back west, William Tecumseh Sherman would strike from Chattanooga into northern Georgia, while Major General Nathaniel P. Banks assailed Mobile, Alabama. In the east, Major General Benjamin "Beast" Butler would lead his Army of the James against Richmond from the southern approaches, while Union troops under Major General Franz Sigel went after valuable supply lines and bases in southwestern Virginia. Grant saved the biggest prize for himself and decided to make his camp with the Army of the Potomac—the tenacious (if unlucky) army that had been bedeviled by Robert E. Lee for nearly two years. In the waning days of April, they would set out to bag the wily Gray Fox and eradicate his formidable Army of Northern Virginia for good.

While Grant's conception for a simultaneous push against Confederate manpower and resources was sound, it looked as if his carefully orchestrated offensive would unravel before the month of May had concluded. At that time, Butler's men were stalemated at Bermuda Hundred, and Sigel's valley army had suffered a humiliating defeat at New Market. Farther west, things were looking just as gloomy. The Army of the Tennessee was defeated at New Hope Church on May 25, and Nathaniel P. Banks—a politician turned soldier who was notorious for being soundly beaten in most of his martial endeavors—completely botched the attempt to take Mobile in what Sherman famously remarked was "one damned blunder from beginning to end." There would be far more blundering before all was said and done.

As galling as these fiascos were, it was Grant himself who was in store for the rudest awakening of them all. Grant led his "Army Group" consisting of Major General George Gordon Meade's Army of the Potomac and Major General Ambrose E. Burnside's independent IX Corps as they crossed Virginia's Rapidan River west of Fredericksburg to entice Lee into open battle. In order to do this, however, Grant had to pass through a tangled wasteland known locally as the Wilderness. The Federals were still negotiating the dense underbrush of this thicket when Lee and his grizzled veterans showed up to give battle. The resulting Battle of the Wilderness raged May 5–6 and provided a severe shock to Grant, whose troops suffered about 20,000 casualties, compared to Lee's 11,000. Old Marse Robert had scored yet another tactical victory, but his opponent showed his mettle when, instead of pulling back to lick his wounds and refit for the next big bloodletting, Grant disengaged from the Wilderness

Lieutenant General Ulysses S. Grant near Cold Harbor, June 1864. *Courtesy of the Library of Congress.*

and continued to press on—this time toward the small hamlet of Spotsylvania Court House. The two armies battered each other May 8–19 in some of the most brutal and horrific fighting the war had yet seen. Grant, who had clearly underestimated Lee, lost a staggering 18,000 men, while his opponent lost 9,500 irreplaceable fighters.

Stride after agonizing stride, inch by bloody inch, Grant's battered host was marching its way ever closer to the Confederate capital and whittling down Lee's vaunted army in the process. As the inexorable march continued to the North Anna River and across the Pamunkey, an ailing Lee found himself unable to wrest the strategic initiative from his opponent's hands. Confederate hopes were momentarily resurrected when the Rebels scored a costly defeat on Grant's army at Cold

Major General George G. Meade led the Army of the Potomac. *Courtesy of the Library of Congress.*

Harbor, just northeast of Richmond. After the now infamous assault on the morning of June 3, the two sides became stalemated yet again. The Cold Harbor Campaign produced 13,000 dead and wounded Federals, while the Army of Northern Virginia lost about 2,500 men. Grant hunkered down June 4–12, consolidated his lines and began to scheme his way out of the deadlock.

With Lee's army and the Chickahominy River interposed between Grant and Richmond, the cigar-smoking chieftain turned his gaze south, toward the city of Petersburg. Five major railways funneled into Petersburg—vital lines coming in from the Shenandoah Valley, southeastern Virginia, and railways connected to blockade-running ports, all of which connected to Richmond. In addition to the railways, Petersburg's road network also supplied the Confederate capital, and important lead works that manufactured the deadly missiles used by Lee's army made for a tempting target.

As Petersburg went, so went Richmond. Thus, on June 6, 1864, Grant informed Benjamin Butler that he was planning on shifting the Army of

the Potomac away from Richmond and toward Petersburg. Butler's Army of the James had been "bottled up" at Bermuda Hundred, a peninsula situated squarely between Richmond and Petersburg, and his engineers had maps that the Army of the Potomac would need to get across the James River. Butler assisted Grant in getting the information he needed and also decided that he would take a gander at seizing Petersburg himself. Thinking that the "Cockade City's" defenses had been weakened by troops being shifted north to Lee's army, Butler sent four brigades of infantry to take the city. In what lives on in local legend as the "Battle of Old Men and Young Boys," a ragtag group of local defense troops and citizens led by former governor of Virginia Henry A. Wise was able to confound the confused and timid Union advance.

The Army of the Potomac fared no better. When Grant slipped away from the killing fields of Cold Harbor, he attempted to take Petersburg starting on June 15—three days later, Lee's men began to arrive, and any opportunity to waltz into Petersburg completely evaporated.

With the Army of Northern Virginia entrenching, "storming Gibraltar would be as easy" as taking Petersburg. That being said, the Confederacy's premier army was in a bad way, and reverting to trench warfare was not an ideal outcome for an army that was suffering a shortage of every resource imaginable. Lee acknowledged as much when he told Jubal Early, "We must destroy this Army of Grant's before he gets to the James River. If he gets there it will become a siege and then it will be a mere question of time."[1]

Both sides were eager to break the deadlock. When the campaign dissolved into siege operations and the summer heat turned the trenches into cesspools of filth and suffering, Grant was offered a pertinent bit of advice: "Hold on with a bulldog grip, and chew and choke as much as possible."[2]

"An Unconditional Surrender"

The man who had given Grant that advice, President Abraham Lincoln, was given plenty of opportunities to heed his own counsel in the spring and summer of 1864. While Father Abraham was not shouldering a musket or directing artillery fire, he was certainly embroiled in conflict aplenty: conflict in his family, his inner circle, with antiwar Democrats (known as "Copperheads") and even with members of his own party. And if this wasn't enough to drive any man to distraction, Lincoln was also facing reelection and had to wage a campaign to convince the American people to keep him in office come November. Lincoln was waging a war while campaigning to make sure that he could keep prosecuting that very same war—at least in the way he saw fit.

"It is a pertinent question often asked in the mind privately, and from one to the other, when is the war to end?" he told a Philadelphia audience on June 16, 1864. "Surely I feel as deep…an interest in this question as any other can, but I do not wish to name a day, or month, or a year when it is to end…We accepted this war for an object, a worthy object, and the war will end when that object is attained. Under God, I hope it never will until that time." This last sentence was potentially controversial, since it implied more blood and treasure to be sacrificed on the altar of the nation. Thus, Lincoln added some rousing encouragement: "Speaking of the present campaign, General Grant is reported to have said, 'I am going through on this line if it takes all summer.'" The Philadelphians in the audience burst forth in cheers and applause, but what would the rest of the country say at this prospect?[3]

With Union military efforts bogging down or resulting in outright failure, Lincoln became unsettled about his prospects for winning a second term. All he had to do was harken back to the midterm elections of 1862, when the rising death toll, new taxes, the suspension of habeas corpus, the draft law and—worst of all in the minds of many voters—the announcement of the Preliminary Emancipation Proclamation resulted in the Republican Party losing 122 seats in the House of Representatives. Two years later, many of those same issues were still raw with the American people, and when it became increasingly evident that the Democrats were going to nominate the ever-popular Major General George B. McClellan as their presidential candidate, there was genuine cause for concern.

Officially, Lincoln was the nominee for the National Union Party, whose platform included, among other planks, a vow "not to compromise with the Rebels, or to offer them any terms of peace except such as may be based upon an unconditional surrender"—a far cry from Democrats' desire for an "honorable peace" that would leave the fate of the slaves in the South ambiguous to say the least.[4]

Even so, Lincoln was not blind to the fact that a peace agreement could theoretically be worked out before Americans went to the polls. Negotiations would have to be handled ever so delicately, but July 1864 saw two different gestures of peace with the Confederate government. The first took place outside American or Confederate soil, across Niagara Falls in Canada. There, the famous founder and editor of the *New York Tribune*, Horace

Greeley, found himself in over his head in dealing with two Confederate negotiators who had no authority to offer any official terms backed by Jefferson Davis's administration. This debacle ended with Greeley feeling duped and humiliated and peace as unreachable as ever.

The second notable peace arbitration took place in Richmond itself, where Colonel James F. Jaquess and James R. Gilmore crossed into the Confederate capital via—of all places—Deep Bottom to discuss peace directly with Jefferson Davis himself. When the Southern head of state drove home the point that there could only be peace if the Confederate States of America was allowed its independence, the handwriting was on the wall, since the Lincoln administration would never accept such an outcome. "Any proposition," the Rail Splitter wrote to the Confederates, "which embraces the restoration of peace, the integrity of the whole Union, and the abandonment of the slavery…will be received and considered by the Executive government of the United States." Any peace proposal lacking those key components would not be contemplated. With the July peace ovations dead on arrival, the North would have to win its victory on the field of battle.[5]

Chapter 2

THE OPPOSING FORCES

"THE ARMY WAS TERRIBLY SHATTERED"

By the spring of 1864, the Army of the Potomac had garnered a reputation for being tough, implacable and steadfast in the face of appalling conditions (to say nothing of appalling leadership). As the war entered its third year, some remarked that the army's personality reflected that of a bulldog—as one of its members observed, "You can whip them time and again, but the next fight they go into, they are in good spirits, and as full of pluck as ever." But as every dog owner can attest, a mutt can be abused and ill treated to the point that it will cower at its own shadow. The meat grinder of the Overland Campaign had begun to produce such a result in these resolute defenders of the republic.[6] Consider the agonizing reflections of a survivor:

> *The army was terribly shattered. It had lost considerably more than half of the troops that crossed the Rapidan on the 3d of May. It had accomplished nothing, save that it had killed, wounded, and captured some 30,000 men of Lee's army. It had carried out its policy of attrition and that was all. It had simply depleted Lee's army. It had neither disintegrated nor demoralized it...The campaign must be pronounced a failure. Of this there can be no real question...The result of this campaign was to reduce our army in numbers and morale out of all proportion with its adversary.*[7]

No group of soldiers embodies the angst of this quote more than the steadfast II Corps, which would be tasked with menacing the capital of the Confederacy during the First Battle of Deep Bottom. One chronicler of the war went so far as to say that "the history of the Second Corps was identical with that of the Army of the Potomac." From Seven Pines to the Bloody Lane of Antietam, Marye's Heights at Fredericksburg to the repulse of Pickett's Charge at Gettysburg, the Clover Leafs had earned a solid reputation as the army's toughest fighters. Whenever a situation was particularly dire, the II Corps, led into battle by its redoubtable commander, Winfield Scott Hancock, would be called on to win the day. Sadly, this reputation would carry over into 1864 with disastrous consequences.[8]

"Played Out!"

The troubles began on the first day of the Battle of the Wilderness. On May 5, 1864, the men of the II Corps experienced something they were not entirely used to: being pushed back. Fighting in the underbrush led to confusion, demoralization and outright panic in some instances. The nightmarish landscape, littered with casualties, took on an added element of hellishness when the woods caught fire, and the men were forced to watch their wounded comrades incinerated before their very eyes. The second day of the battle went no better, and the tone was set for a campaign that was simply more difficult than any other that the boys could recall. The corps would see action throughout the Spotsylvania Campaign, most notably at the "Mule Shoe" on May 12 and the Harris Farm on May 19. Despite the heavy combat that the corps was enduring, morale remained high as the campaign sputtered toward Richmond. All of that changed at Cold Harbor.

Following the fighting along the North Anna River, the II Corps was forced to endure an agonizing night march on the evening of June 1–2 that exacerbated the men's growing sense of frustration and fatigue. To make matters worse, a guide who was sent to lead the corps to its position on the Union left flank got lost, so that by the time they arrived in their sector of the Union lines, Hancock's men were simply played out. Because of this, Grant decided to postpone his main assault at Cold Harbor until June 3, 1864—a day that would certainly live in infamy in the lore of the II Corps for the remainder of its existence. The morning attack on the Confederate entrenchments was swift, violent and completely lopsided. One of Hancock's staff officers offered a brutally terse description of the assault: "Scarcely twenty-two minutes from the time the signal was given, the repulse of the corps was complete. Three thousand men had fallen." What historians have since called "Cold Harbor syndrome" would haunt the corps as it pressed forward to Petersburg.[9]

From June 15 to June 18, Hancock's men were involved in the initial attempts by the Army of the Potomac to seize Petersburg—a task that historians agree they should have been able to accomplish. But by this point, the men had been marching and fighting for more than forty days, and the strain was taking a tremendous toll. By June 18, when an evening attack was ordered against a strong enemy fortification, the men simply refused to attack. "Played out!" they shouted. Four days later, they suffered what the official chronicler of the II Corps called "the most humiliating episode in the experience of the…corps." In a joint effort with the VI Corps to cut the Weldon Railroad, the battered corps was stampeded by a Confederate flank attack that resulted in the loss of 1,700 prisoners—more than the corps had lost at Antietam, Fredericksburg and Chancellorsville combined. As the operations around Petersburg settled into a stagnant siege, the II Corps was broken in spirit and body, and the generals who led it were faced with a crisis in manpower.[10]

"THE IDEAL AMERICAN SOLDIER"

Winfield Scott Hancock was a born fighter. Named after War of 1812 hero Winfield Scott, he entered life in February 1824 in the Commonwealth of Pennsylvania. At the fresh age of sixteen, he was enrolled in the United States Military Academy at West Point, where he learned the finer details of soldiering with fellow classmates Alexander Hays, Ulysses S. Grant and Ambrose E. Burnside, among others. Four years later, he graduated eighteenth in his class. When war was declared with Mexico, Hancock showed flashes of the brilliance to come and won a brevet promotion for his heroic exploits at the Battle of Churubusco.

When the Civil War broke out, Hancock led a brigade in the Army of the Potomac and saw his first action during the Peninsula Campaign. On May 5, 1862, during the Battle of Williamsburg, his leadership was described as "superb" by Major General George B. McClellan; from that time forward, his nickname was "Hancock the Superb." His star on the rise, Hancock led

Major General Winfield S. Hancock.
Courtesy of the Library of Congress.

a division at the Battle of Antietam and was promoted to major general of volunteers in November 1862. He led his men in the calamitous attack on Marye's Heights at the Battle of Fredericksburg the following month and was wounded in the abdomen. At Chancellorsville, he received a second wound while conducting a brilliant holding action at the Chancellor House clearing, where he held Lee's army at bay long enough for the rest of the Army of the Potomac to withdraw. Following this stinging Union defeat, General Darius Couch, who had commanded the II Corps, left. Hancock became the new commander.

The Battle of Gettysburg was Hancock's finest hour to date, but it would prove costly for the young corps commander. On July 1, 1863, Hancock was given command of I, III and XI Corps following the death of John Reynolds. The next day, Hancock played a key role in averting disaster following General Dan Sickle's blunder at the Peach Orchard. On July 3, his men helped repulse Pickett's Charge, during which Hancock received his third battlefield wound in as many campaigns. And a ghastly wound it was—one that would have far-reaching repercussions for Hancock's remaining months with the Army of the Potomac. While seated on his horse directing troops, a bullet pierced the pommel of his saddle, carrying bits of wood and a saddle nail into his groin along with the bullet. The stricken general was in excruciating pain, yet he refused to be moved from the field until the battle was over.

Hancock would not rejoin the II Corps until late March 1864, and when he returned, he was still not completely healed from his wound. He had gained weight due to being immobile for many months, and this only exacerbated the pain he felt while riding a horse, which he described as "agony." The Overland Campaign showed the fault lines in Hancock's sterling reputation, and the early failures around Petersburg only made the situation worse. Following the war, John Newton, who had commanded the Union I Corps shortly before it was disbanded, said of the general who had once been known as "the Superb": "Hancock is not the soldier that some of them are. He is a good soldier but not a great one...He had the luck of inheriting other men's deeds." Even so, most of the men under his command adored him to the end, stating, "To us he was the ideal American soldier...the embodiment of the highest type of manhood that can be developed under our form of government."[11]

When Hancock returned to his beloved corps, there were four seasoned divisions under his command. By late June 1864, the command had been so whittled down by severe casualties that the corps was consolidated into three divisions, and it was these three divisions that would square off against the Confederates at Deep Bottom. The division commanders were, respectively, Brigadier General Francis C. Barlow, Major General John Gibbon and Brigadier General Gershom Mott.

"A Highly Independent Newsboy"

Francis Channing Barlow was only twenty-six years old at the outbreak of the American Civil War. Barlow was a bit of a *wunderkind*, having graduated first in his class at Harvard and achieved marked success as a lawyer and writer for the *New York Tribune*. He spent part of his youth at the famed utopian commune Brook Farm, ran in the same social circles as Nathaniel Hawthorne and Ralph Waldo Emerson and even tutored a young student named Robert Gould Shaw. On April 20, 1861, Barlow married Arabella Griffith, a fellow sophisticate ten years his senior. The next day, he went off to war.[12]

Amazingly, Barlow began his military career as a private in a New York militia unit. After a brief stint as a ninety-day volunteer, Barlow reenlisted and entered the army as a lieutenant colonel in the 61st New York. Although he had no prior military experience whatsoever, Barlow quickly showed himself adept in the arts of war during the Peninsula Campaign, during which he was promoted to full colonel. Barlow frequently expressed his displeasure with the officers above him and was prone to bouts of misgivings about his career. Still, his fervor to see the rebellion crushed kept him at the head of his troops, leading with an iron hand. At Antietam, Barlow sustained a painful wound in the groin while fearlessly pushing the Confederates out of the famed Sunken Road. The young colonel

Brigadier General Francis C. Barlow.
Courtesy of the Library of Congress.

was out of commission until 1863, when he rejoined the army as a brigade commander in the hapless XI Corps. He was with the corps when it was smashed by "Stonewall" Jackson's flank attack at the Battle of Chancellorsville, although his brigade saw minimal action. Two months later, at Gettysburg, Barlow would not be so fortunate. On July 1, 1863, Barlow—now a division commander—was severely defeated along with the rest of the XI Corps during the engagement. As he tried to rally his men on what is now known as "Barlow's Knoll," the youthful officer was hit three times and fell into the hands of the enemy. He was so grievously wounded that it was assumed he would not survive, and he was promoted to brigadier general before his supposed death. But Barlow was not about to die with the war unfinished, and in early 1864, he was back in the saddle.

Through some wrangling from his friend Nelson Miles, Barlow was brought into the II Corps as the head of the First Division. The cleanshaven general, with his penchant for wearing loose-fitting clothing and checkered shirts, was described as looking like a "highly independent newsboy," but he quickly won over his men. The upcoming series of battles would test Barlow like nothing ever had, and his performance in the Overland Campaign mirrored that of the II Corps. On May 20, 1864, as the army moved toward the North Anna, Barlow confessed in a letter to his brother, "I long for this damned Campaign to be over." One month later, he expressed that he was "fully resolved as one can be of anything in the future to resign when this active Campaign is over."[13]

Whittled down by the unremitting stresses of nonstop fighting, Barlow was showing signs of cracking. Little did he know that the cruelest blow of all would come during the expedition north of the James.

"The Most American of Americans"

Commanding Hancock's Second Division was John Gibbon. Born in Philadelphia, Gibbon's family moved to Charlotte, North Carolina, when he was a young boy. In 1842, he received an appointment to the United States Military Academy, where he was part of the class of 1847. His chief contribution before the war was as an artillery instructor at West Point and as the author of *The Artillerist's Manual,* a text that would be widely read and used by both sides. When the Civil War broke out, the Gibbon family faced a crisis that was repeated in thousands of households throughout the broken nation: three of John's bothers and a soon-to-be-famous cousin, J. Johnston Pettigrew, cast their loyalties with the Southern Confederacy. Even his wife, who was from the secessionist hotbed of Baltimore, had Southern sympathies. In spite of all of this, Gibbon—whom Theodore Lyman would characterize as "the most American of Americans"—upheld the oath he had taken to the United States.[14]

Gibbon's first assignment was, naturally, as chief of artillery for Major General Irvin McDowell. In May 1862, he tried his hand at the infantry after his promotion to brigadier general. He received command of a brigade of western troops he soon drilled into some of the most tenacious fighters in the Army of the Potomac. Their first taste of combat was at the Brawner Farm during the Second Manassas Campaign. One month later, at Turner's Gap, General Joseph Hooker would give Gibbon's men a famous nickname: the "Iron Brigade."

The brigade was heavily engaged in the famous cornfield at Antietam, where Gibbon reverted to his old ways and personally manned an artillery piece. He was promoted to division command before the Fredericksburg Campaign. At a place called the Slaughter Pen Farm, he faced James H. Lane's

Brigadier General John Gibbon. *Courtesy of the Library of Congress.*

North Carolina Brigade, in which two of his Confederate brothers served. Gibbon was wounded in the wrist by a shell fragment and did not rejoin the army until the spring of 1863.

He commanded the Second Division of the II Corps at Gettysburg, where he and his men played a significant part in the repulse of Pickett's Charge. Gibbon was wounded in the shoulder during this climactic fight and was fortunate enough to have a chance to attend the dedication of Gettysburg's national cemetery, where Abraham Lincoln delivered the Gettysburg Address. By the spring of 1864, Gibbon was back in command of his old division and led his men through the hellish nightmare of the Overland Campaign and the attempts at Petersburg.[15]

"One of the Most Prominent Soldiers of New Jersey"

Heading up the Third Division in July 1864 was Gershom Mott, remembered as "one of the most prominent soldiers of New Jersey during the War of the Rebellion." Mott was the grandson of a Revolutionary War hero and received his education at the Trenton Academy, as opposed to West Point, where so many of his comrades were schooled before the war. Still, Mott received a commission during the Mexican-American War. He was working at a bank in 1861, and following the firing on Fort Sumter, he was appointed lieutenant colonel of the 5th New Jersey Infantry. He and his regiment fought well on the Peninsula, and shortly after the Battle of Williamsburg, he was promoted to full colonel and given command of the 6th New Jersey. He was commended for bravery at Seven Pines and was severely wounded at Second Manassas, which caused him to miss Antietam and Fredericksburg.[16]

He returned to the Army of the Potomac in time to lead a brigade in the III Corps at the Battle of Chancellorsville, where he was wounded again, causing him to miss the Battle of Gettysburg. Mott returned to duty in the fall of 1863 in time for the Bristoe and Mine Run Campaigns. He commanded the Fourth Division of the II Corps during the Overland Campaign. His failure to support Upton's Division at Spotsylvania Court House led to the division being disbanded, in spite of severe protests from Mott. This disastrous battlefield performance also led to distrust by Hancock and Barlow. Mott was humiliated at being demoted to

Brigadier General Gershom Mott. *Courtesy of the Library of Congress.*

brigade command, but when Major General David B. Birney left to command the X Corps, Mott was given the Third Division, which he led "in gallant style."[17]

"A BROWN, CHUNKY LITTLE CHAP"

Major General Philip Sheridan. *Courtesy of the Library of Congress.*

Major General Philip Henry Sheridan was described by President Lincoln as "[a] brown, chunky little chap, with a long body, short legs, not enough neck to hang him, and such long arms that if his ankles itch he can scratch them without stooping." His personality more than made up for his appearance.

The thirty-three-year-old former infantry commander came east with Grant and took command of the Army of the Potomac's cavalry in late March 1864. When the spring offensive kicked off in May, Sheridan proved adept at infuriating George Gordon Meade but lacked the finesse of a truly great cavalry commander. By the time of the Deep Bottom expedition, Sheridan's record was spotty at best.

"WE HOPE TO DRIVE THEM BACK AGAIN"

For ardent Confederate nationalists, Lee's Army of Northern Virginia had almost come to symbolize the nation itself by the summer of 1864. While white Southerners certainly faced the same war weariness and disillusion that their Northern counterparts were experiencing, a surprising number of Confederates found themselves hopeful that the opening of the spring campaign season would mark the beginning of their march to final victory. Judith Brockenbrough McGuire, a clerk in the Confederate Commissary Department in Richmond, wrote in her diary entry of April 25, 1864:

> *The enemy threatens Richmond, and is coming against it with an immense arm. They boast that they can and will have it this summer; but with the help of God, we hope to drive them back again. Our Government is making every effort to defeat them. I don't think that anyone doubts our ability to do it; but the awful loss of life necessary upon the fights is what we dread.*[18]

Even when the Yankee army continued to sidestep its way closer and closer to Richmond, many Southern newspapers portrayed Grant's extremely aggressive action as desperation. Hindsight being as it is, this effusive confidence can be mystifying. However, "without knowledge of the outcome…Confederate optimism seems rational given the course of the war to this point," wrote historian Aaron Sheehan-Dean. "The confidence of mid-1864, even shadowed by Lee's retreat through central Virginia, added to the psychological stake Virginians held in independence." The same held true of civilians throughout the Confederacy.[19]

"We Are Not Near Whiped"

The army that protected the Confederate capital that spring had taken heavy losses, but it was still as dangerous and lethal as ever. The Army of Northern Virginia entered the Overland Campaign with 66,140 men, and throughout the heavy fighting around Richmond and Petersburg, that number had dwindled to 52,325 by June 30—a number not entirely reflective of the scale of loss, considering that the army had been reinforced throughout the campaign. If McGuire and her compatriots were hopeful of Confederate independence being achieved in 1864, the men who fought under Lee were all but certain of it. Before the Overland Campaign kicked off, one Confederate wrote home that "Genl. Lee's old army…is now generally considered to be in better spirits & health, also better armed equipped &c, than at any previous time during the war." A soldier in Kershaw's brigade, which would be heavily involved in the upcoming fighting at Deep Bottom, similarly wrote that "there is non hoo have boore more of the hardships and are still willing to endure them rather than Submit to Such men as are Seeking to destroy us and all we have…we are not near whiped." When the campaign bogged down around Petersburg and soldiers had to grow accustomed to life in the trenches, this confidence abated a bit—after all, it was a siege conducted by Grant that had reduced the stronghold of Vicksburg one year previous—but their faith in their cause and commander was still remarkably high.[20]

While much ink has been spilled on the devotion that the common soldier of the Army of Northern Virginia felt toward Robert E. Lee, one quote from July 1864 is especially illustrative. A twenty-three-year-old artillerist wrote of Lee that "he should certainly have entire control of all military operations throughout the Confederate States." While this sentiment was quite common in the ranks, the next sentence may have raised a few eyebrows in the Confederate war department: "In fact I should like to see him King or Dictator. He is one of the few great men who ever lived, who could be trusted."[21] If Lee was the kingly defender of Confederate aspirations, the officers who managed Lee's three infantry corps were not quite as regal.

Lieutenant General James "Pete" Longstreet of the First Corps was the most experienced and trustworthy of Lee's subordinates in the spring of 1864. However, he was severely wounded on the second day of the Battle of the Wilderness. Heading up the Third Corps was A.P. Hill, who suffered from failing health and a streak of impetuosity that would follow him until his death outside Petersburg in 1865. Hill's reckless attack on the Union II Corps at Bristoe Station in October 1863 is but one example of his failure to display discernment—a failure that cost him 1,800 needless casualties. Rounding out Lee's corps commanders on the eve of the Overland Campaign was Richard Stoddert Ewell, head of the Second Corps, formerly under the inimitable "Stonewall" Jackson. Like Longstreet, Ewell would not survive the campaign, although for much different reasons.

General Robert E. Lee. *Courtesy of the Library of Congress.*

On May 6, 1864, Ewell continued a bad habit of disappointing Robert E. Lee, much as he had at Gettysburg in 1863. His failure to attack the flank of the Union VI Corps, coupled with what Lee viewed as similar failures to capitalize on opportunities to defeat the Federals during the fighting around Spotsylvania Court House, made Ewell a marked man, and on June 15, 1864, "Old Bald Head" was given command of the Department of Richmond. The Second Corps would go to Jubal Early. The demotion stung Ewell, who found himself going from command of some of the best shock troops in the entire Confederacy to the leader of a few thousand reserve units, heavy artillery battalions and local defense troops, the latter of which "were called out on occasions of necessity, and

Lieutenant General Richard S. Ewell. After disappointing Lee one too many times, Ewell was stripped of command of the Second Corps and placed in charge of the Department of Richmond. *Courtesy of the Library of Congress.*

could only be spared for a few days at a time." Although he could not have known it at the time, Ewell would soon find himself in a critical role defending Richmond during the First Battle of Deep Bottom.[22]

Assisting Ewell with the defense of Richmond would be four other principal commanders. Lieutenant General Richard H. Anderson would top this list. A South Carolinian by birth, Anderson was a West Point graduate and Mexican-American War veteran. Anderson took over for Longstreet as head of the First Corps when Longstreet was wounded. Anderson was a rare bird in the Army of Northern Virginia in that he did not engage in flagrant self-promotion in the way that many of his cohorts did. His biographer noted that he was "[o]ne utterly without that self-assertion which alas! seems so necessary to win recognition and gain the plaudits of mankind."[23]

Major General Joseph B. Kershaw was a division commander in Anderson's First Corps. He, too, was a South Carolinian and was a prewar politician and lawyer. Kershaw was also relatively rare in that he was a so-called political general who blossomed into a great commander of troops. As one biographer noted, Kershaw was a "striking example of the citizen-soldier, who with little military background developed into a wholly dependable… brigade and division commander."[24]

Serving under Kershaw, Benjamin Grubb Humphreys was a Mississippian whose military career was seemingly sidelined when he was kicked out of the United States Military Academy at West Point following a cadet riot on Christmas Eve 1826. When war broke out, Humphreys was able to redeem himself by raising a company of Mississippi troops dubbed the "Sunflower Guards" that would be commanded by William Barksdale. Humphreys was known as a fierce fighter filled with "zeal, courage, and coolness."[25]

Martin Witherspoon Gary would command troops in the Department of Richmond who would be heavily involved in the Deep Bottom affair.

Gary, another college flunky (he was kicked out of South Carolina College for his involvement in the great "Biscuit Rebellion"), was a high-strung cavalry leader who received his schooling in the arts of war from Wade Hampton. Known as "the Bald Eagle," Gary had a violent temperament but was also described as a "thoroughbred fighter, cool and deliberate, with great good sense." He and his men would leave their mark on operations north of the James River.[26]

And so it was that the two great armies of the Eastern Theater settled into a siege that, unbeknownst to them, would last nine months and cost more than sixty thousand casualties. From the moment that the first Union shovel broke Rebel soil, Grant searched for a way to break the deadlock. He quickly decided on a strategy whereby he would threaten Richmond whenever he launched an effort at Petersburg. In early June, however, he was still in need of a place from which to launch these forays against the Rebel capital. On June 19, he realized that the answer to this dilemma lay at a place called Deep Bottom.

Chapter 3

The Bridgehead Is Established

"What Do These Moves Mean?"

The war came to Deep Bottom at the end of June, within days of the abysmal Federal efforts to take the city of Petersburg. On June 18, 1864, Major General George Gordon Meade's final series of assaults on the Cockade City failed. The next day would mark the official beginning on the Siege of Petersburg, as well as the commencement of Grant's determined effort to break it. With this goal in mind, the lieutenant general boarded a ship with Major General Benjamin F. Butler to seek out a location to open up simultaneous operations against Richmond. Grant's staff officer Lieutenant Colonel Cyrus Comstock recalled going with Grant, Butler and "one or two others up James river to see a site for crossing & bridgehead on other side." The group determined that Deep Bottom was the most suitable location.[27]

A self-descriptive term used to refer to an area of the James River eleven miles southeast of Richmond, Deep Bottom was located at a horseshoe-shaped bend in the river known as Jones Neck. Since it was convenient to the Bermuda Hundred Peninsula, where the Army of the James was currently operating, Deep Bottom was selected for this crossing point to "divide the attention of the enemy's troops, and to confuse them as to whether to expect an attack upon Richmond or Petersburg," according to Grant's aide, Horace Porter.[28]

After returning to headquarters, Grant ordered Butler to

*send a brigade of not less than 2,000 men to-morrow night to seize, hold,
and fortify the most commanding and defensible ground that can be found
north of James River, and so near the river that, with the protection of the
gun-boats and their own strength, they can always get back to Bermuda
Hundred if attacked by superior numbers. Connect the two banks of the
river by a pontoon bridge near Deep Bottom.*

Meade then directed Brigadier General Henry W. Benham of the
Army of the Potomac's engineer brigade to furnish bridging material to
General Butler.[29]

Butler selected Brigadier General Godfrey Weitzel to oversee the
operation, which would include a river crossing, the construction of
a pontoon bridge and the building of fortifications to protect the new
bridgehead. Weitzel immediately contacted General Benham and put
in a request for thirty-five pontoon boats, one hundred pontoniers "in
charge of an able officer" and enough material to build a bridge seven
hundred feet long. Benham responded that Weitzel would have everything
he needed by 8:00 a.m. the next morning.[30]

Brigadier General Robert S. Foster of the X Corps was chosen to lead
this small expedition. Butler ordered Foster to "hold your command in
readiness to move at a moment's notice, with two days' rations and 100
rounds of ammunition, to occupy a point on the north side of the James
River near Deep Bottom." Foster's men were to be ferried across the river in
pontoon boats, and once they hit the shore, they were told to begin digging
trenches immediately. The engineers tasked to build the bridge would begin
construction once Foster's men were securely in place. Butler made sure to
mention to Foster that he and his men were to "hold at all hazards till the
bridge is complete." Butler clued Foster in to the fact that "the object of
this movement is to gain a permanent foothold on the north bank of the
James River." An additional 1,800 so-called Hundred Days Men (volunteers
recruited for one hundred days of service) would be sent to Weitzel to provide
manual labor.[31]

Foster was assigned Colonel Harris M. Plaisted's 3rd Brigade, consisting of
the 10th Connecticut, 100th New York, 24th Massachusetts and 11th Maine.
Also coming along on the expedition were the 85th Pennsylvania and the
39th Illinois of Colonel Joshua B. Howell's 1st Brigade. Sections of the 1st
Connecticut Light Battery and 5th Battery New Jersey Light Artillery

Brigadier General Robert S. Foster. A hard-fighting Indiana native, Foster was tasked with leading the troops who would establish the Deep Bottom bridgehead on June 20, 1864. *Courtesy of the Library of Congress.*

provided artillery support, and a detachment of the 1st New York Mounted Rifles accompanied the expedition.[32]

At 5:00 p.m. on June 20, Foster's command prepared to move out. A soldier in the 85th Pennsylvania recalled that "the men were congratulating themselves that they would have a good night's rest, as the enemy was quiet in front, when they received orders to get ready for an expedition, with 100 rounds of cartridges, two days rations, in light marching orders." The soldiers speculated about where they were headed—"some said to make an attack & charge the rebel trenches in front, others to go on a secret expedition," recalled a soldier in the 24th Massachusetts. When the men were formed, Foster's column marched three miles through intense heat and dust to Jones' Neck, where the pontoons had already been assembled.[33]

Weitzel knew that Confederate pickets were only three hundred yards away and was very apprehensive as the operation began to unfold. As he later reported, "Immediately after dark the pontoon boats were brought to the James River…silently unloaded and placed in the stream, and safely and quietly landed 1,400 men at the designated spot in less than thirty minutes after embarkation." Once on the north side of the river, the wooded bluffs would have to be scaled and a perimeter established before any further work could continue. When the first soldiers made it to the top of the bluff, a chilling sight met them: recently abandoned Confederate earthworks.[34]

By 11:00 p.m., all of Foster's men were on the far side of the river and ready to get to work. Weitzel divided his men up to ensure that the work went quickly, placing "500 men with shovels, 200 with picks, and 200 with axes" to work, with "a regiment placed on picket in advance of all." The work went quickly, and a soldier in Company D, 11th Maine, would later recall:

> Deep Bottom was a well wooded bluff when we seized it, but 'twas bare enough before many days, so vigorously were axes plied by the men of our regiment, and while they were renewing their youth as axemen, fatigue parties from regiments more used to the spade were throwing up a strong line of works, batteries connected by infantry parapets and with outlying rifle pits, forming when completed and with gunboats anchored on the flanks, a practically impregnable "bridge head" for the ponton bridge now laid across from the south bank of the James to Deep Bottom.[35]

Meanwhile, on the south side of the river, the engineers "divided into details to carry the string-pieces, to place them in position on the boats, to bring plank, to lay them in place," all of which was done with "wonderful celerity and precision, so that a little after midnight the bridge was complete."

The upper pontoon bridge at Deep Bottom. Grant's original plan called for the infantry to cross the James at this point, while the cavalry crossed at the lower bridge. *Courtesy of the Library of Congress.*

The work continued all through the night, and the Confederates were none the wiser. Weitzel was rightfully proud to report that "the pontoon bridge, roads, and approaches were all completed before daybreak." One soldier in Company H, 100th New York, was pleased at the night's work but was confounded by the need for such a fortification in the first place. Writing to his parents on June 23, Edward Cook reflected, "This is a new…move on the part of Gen. Grant. No one can conjecture its meaning or significance… What do these moves mean?"[36]

Confused or not, by the early morning hours of June 21, the Deep Bottom bridgehead was in place and expanding. At 1:15 a.m., Foster proudly reported, "I have established my picket-line without resistance. My intrenching and slashing parties are at work."[37]

It would remain a thorn in the side of the Confederates for the rest of the war.

"I Don't Think the Movement Amounts to Much"

Word came to Confederate headquarters early on the morning of June 21, 1864, reporting the newest Federal threat to the safety of the Confederate capital. Robert E. Lee's oldest son, Brigadier General George Washington Custis Lee, newly appointed commander of the troops east of Richmond, reported to his father that an enemy force of unknown size was at Deep Bottom. Colonel Walter Taylor of the elder Lee's staff wrote back and asked for an estimate of the size of the enemy force and informed him that the Third Corps brigade of John Rodgers Cooke—brother-in-law of the recently deceased J.E.B. Stuart—was nearby and could move to his support if necessary. Meanwhile, Lieutenant Colonel J.M. Maury, commanding the garrison at Chaffin's Bluff, opined to Colonel Taylor, "I don't think the movement amounts to much."[38]

Confusion reigned as the Confederates north of the James tried to ascertain the situation. Ewell, who had only taken command of the Department of Richmond the week before, did not even have a proper staff to assist him with gathering and reporting crucial information. The former corps commander could only muster about four thousand second-rate troops, many of whom were heavy artillerists or clerks from the Richmond Defense Troops. The situation was even more dire when compared to what was happening elsewhere on the chessboard of war— that very morning, Grant had sent troops to seize the Weldon Railroad, a vital supply line near Petersburg. Brigadier General Lee was eventually able to report back to his father on the twenty-first that the "enemy's force is about 2,000, chiefly infantry, some cavalry." An anxious Ewell looked at these figures and appealed to Robert E. Lee, "In view of these reports and facts, an increase of force on this side of the river may be necessary."[39]

Meanwhile, the Federals continued to dig in and expand their toehold north of the James. The 10th Connecticut and 24th Massachusetts kept careful watch over the area, leaving the rest of Foster's men to dig in. At 5:25 a.m., Foster sent word that the bridge had just been completed and that, so far, the Confederates had left him alone. Soon the remainder of Foster's men were across and digging in. They had artillery emplacement set up early in the morning, and after securing a place for the gunners, they continued to expand the bridgehead. A diarist in the 85th Pennsylvania recorded:

Immediately after daybreak the Regiment crossed the James River to the north bank, on a pontoon-bridge thrown across the river during the night, and heavy details were immediately put to work fortifying the approaches to the bridge on the north side of the James.[40]

The detachment of the 1st New York Mounted Rifles had a brief tussle with the 24th Virginia Cavalry before picketing the area near the Grover House, where it could deal with any Confederate threats issuing from Chaffin's Bluff. While the expanding *tête de pont* became more secure with each swing of an axe, the Federals were extremely vulnerable to artillery. If the Rebels could maneuver some cannons into position, they could potentially destroy the nascent Federal bridgehead.

By the end of the month, the Rebels would put this new approach into practice.

"I Think It Is a Very Foolish Thing"

Lee dispatched Henry Heth's Third Corps division to the north side of the James on June 22, and his foot soldiers entrenched at New Market Heights, with his right at the Aiken Farm and his left at Chaffin's Bluff. With Heth were two battalions of artillery from the Confederate Second Corps, which had been left behind from that corps' foray into the Shenandoah Valley. Commanded by Colonel Thomas H. Carter, they included four massive twenty-pound Parrott rifles under the command of Captain Archibald Graham. The first day resulted in no substantial gains for the Confederates. Heth reported to Lee's Headquarters that he "did not think it prudent to attack the enemy" because of the presence of large Federal gunboats. Furthermore, "Colonel Carter could find no position from which he could accomplish anything."[41]

Sporadic skirmishing would take place for the next few days, and Foster would become increasingly nervous about his tenuous position, especially as Grant seemed content to leave the bridgehead in place while putting most of his effort behind another attack at Petersburg. With both Grant and Lee occupied with the events transpiring at Petersburg in the last week of June, Lee ordered Ewell to implement a strategy of harassment, with Carter's guns now stepping onto the stage to harass the soldiers at the bridgehead and the Union shipping that was bringing Grant's and Butler's armies the vital supplies they needed.

Foster's Headquarters at Deep Bottom, sketched by William Waud. A handwritten note on the back reads: "[B]etween 3 & 4 miles from Malvern Hills and on the same side of the James River showing the Pontoon bridge & the double end gun boats protecting one of his flanks. Gen Foster has an entrenched position here which is likely to become the base of operations for movements of importance. When the object of this position is more fully developed I will send other sketches of it. W.W." *Courtesy of the Library of Congress.*

With this in mind, the men of the 1st Rockbridge Artillery set to work digging in near New Market Heights. On June 24, Private Thomas M. Wade Jr. complained, "We have been working night & day on fortifications to fire at gunboats in the James River. I think it is a very foolish thing & so does the captain [Graham] but the order emanates from Col. Carter and must be obeyed." Colonel Carter positioned Graham's four Parrott rifles behind the newly completed works at the foot of New Market Heights in order to harass Foster's men at the bridgehead, as well as any Union ships coming up the river. Gary's men were in support. Their mission would begin the next morning.[42]

At 7:00 a.m. on the morning of June 29, Graham's Battery fired its first shots from two thousand yards. Its target was the side-wheel steamer USS *Hunchback*, a converted ferryboat stationed on the river to protect the Deep Bottom bridgehead. The *Hunchback* was supported by a single-turret monitor, the USS *Saugus*. For the entire day, Graham's Battery traded shots with the enemy ships, striking the *Hunchback* in the port wheelhouse and hitting another hapless wooden vessel that was passing by. The *Hunchback* and *Saugus* pounded the new earthworks that Graham's men had dug, and every massive shell they fired seemed to land squarely within them. Yet the artillery duel raged on.

The next day, the lopsided contest was renewed by the Federals, who brought up the USS *Mendota* and the USS *Agawam* to add their firepower to the shelling of the New Market Line. As they began to blaze away, the Confederates offered no reply, causing the Yankee sailors to scratch their heads and wonder what their prey was up to. As it turned out, Graham's men had moved overnight to a position closer to the river at Tilghman's Gate. When a Frenchman living at the nearby Allen Farm informed Lieutenant Joseph Fyffe of the *Hunchback* of this new development, the Federals sailed to this new position and opened fire, prompting an immediate response from Graham's gunners. The Rockbridge Artillerymen fired at the ships and lobbed a number of shells into the infantry camps at Deep Bottom for good measure before shifting their position once again.[43]

This two-day exchange worried Rear Admiral Samuel P. Lee, who reported, "The importance of holding our position at Deep Bottom is obvious. Without doing so our communications are cut there, and our wooden vessels can not remain above that point, and the monitors would be alone and exposed." Private Sidney A. Lake, Company C, 100th New York, who had watched the affair from the bridgehead, was not nearly as concerned. Writing home on July 1, Lake related:

> The rebs planted A battery up in the woods near here and fired on the boats but to no purpose. A small wooden boat fired considerable but could not drive it off. But A Monitor came down and soon silenced it. They might [have] shelled us out of camp as easy as not, for the camp is 10 rods in front of our breast works and in A very exposed position. But they could not see us and probably thought we were in side the works, so did not try it.

June 30, however, would mark the end of Ewell's attempt to drive away the Yankees with Carter's guns alone.[44]

A disappointed Lee wrote to Ewell and said, "I had hoped that Colonel Carter would have been able to have annoyed, if not injured, [the enemy's] transports on the river…Please see if anything can be done to drive the enemy from the north bank and interrupt his communications, &c." On the evening of June 30, Brigadier General James Lane's Brigade, under the command of Brigadier General James Conner, and McGowan's Brigade left the Petersburg front and marched to the Outer Line north of Chaffin's

Bluff. They joined a disparate force of artillery, cavalry and the Richmond City Battalion. This freed up Heth's men to return to the Petersburg lines.[45]

As June turned to July, activity along the Deep Bottom front settled into a predictable routine. A soldier in the 100th New York was ecstatic to report that "we had the best of spring water bubbling from the earth…and most of our front and right of the picket line, was in the woods, a welcome shade during the very warm days of July and August." For the Confederates in McGowan's Brigade, life wasn't nearly so serene. The brigade historian wrote of their time at New Market Heights:

> *We had no tents, except the scraps of Yankee flies; we were fed on wretched bacon, wormy peas, and corn meal, with a small sprinkling of coffee; we lacked shoes and clothing; we were exposed to great heat and kept constantly on some sort of duty; yet we constructed arbors of branches, picked blackberries, smoked pipes (when we had tobacco), and felt very comfortable indeed.*

Attention shifted away from Richmond and Petersburg as Lee dispatched forces to the Shenandoah Valley to threaten Washington, D.C. This sideshow prevented Grant from attacking the weakened Deep Bottom front when the time was opportune for a breakthrough there.[46]

Activity at Deep Bottom would not pick up again until the last week of July.

"I Do Not Like the Continuance of the Enemy on the North Side of the James River"

With a shortage of manpower preventing Robert E. Lee from sending a force large enough to raze Foster's bridgehead, he turned to the possibility of using another method to harass the Union flotilla on the James: mines. Called "torpedoes" in nineteenth-century military parlance, Lee wrote to Ewell in early July, expressing that "I have been anxious for some time to accomplish this." Due to a comedy of errors, however, this scheme was not put into practice until later in the month. While the Confederate Torpedo Bureau had the mines to give to Ewell's forces, it had no boats, oars or men with which to place them in the river. Frustrated, Ewell reverted to using Graham's Battery to damage the Federals on the north bank.[47]

On July 6, an exasperated Lee told Ewell, "I do not like the continuance of the enemy on the north side of the James River and the maintenance

Another wartime sketch of Deep Bottom, by Alfred Waud. Union camps are visible in the background, and the boat shown is most likely the USS *Mendota*. *Courtesy of the Library of Congress.*

of the pontoon bridge at Deep Bottom. I believe his force is not very large, and desire you to see if it cannot be driven away, and the bridge destroyed." Ewell got the message, and on July 13, Graham's four Parrott rifles were put back into action with a vengeance. For the next week, Graham's gunners would play a cat-and-mouse game with both the army and navy, slipping into one position to lob a few shells at a gunboat and then sliding into another position to shell Foster's men. Typical of the damage was what one member of the 24th Massachusetts recorded in his diary for July 14: Graham's men opened fire, and their shells killed "a horse and six men" on the *Mendota*.[48]

"I Think It Must Be Much Further on This Poor Horse"

On July 19, the Rockbridge Artillerists were able to even lob their deadly missiles directly into Foster's own headquarters. W.H. Merriam of the *New York Herald* was at headquarters when the barrage began at 7:00 a.m. Merriam stated that the fusillade lasted "for upwards of an hour" and that "the range was so accurate as to compel the inmates to change their base several times." The journalist also reported that "several large fragments of shell passed directly into the tent of the General, while yet other shot literally cut to pieces the trees and the foliage immediately surrounding the tents." Fortunately, no men were lost, although P.A. Davis of Foster's staff watched from his tent as his horse was felled by a shell fragment.

At 8:00 a.m., the Confederate artillery turned its sights to the Union flotilla and began banging away at the gunboats. Its first target was the *Mendota*, and Merriam watched from the shore as a single shot took out six men, while another hit the crow's nest and splintered the mast. A few hours later, none other than Grant and Butler, along with various members of their staff, showed up to consult with Foster, while the artillery exchange took place on the water nearby. After the party looked over a map, Grant "smoked his segar and read Richmond papers while on the picket line and under fire, with that stubborn and never absent imperturbability for which he is noted wherever he is known." Meanwhile, Butler "was intent on seeing as much of the rebels as possible." When the party was ready to leave, Grant apparently mounted the wrong horse by accident. The poor animal belonged to a staff officer and was suffering from laminitis, a painful hoof disease. After trying to ride the animal, Grant asked how far it was to Richmond.

"About ten miles," a staff officer replied.

Dismounting the horse, Grant replied, "I think it must be much further on this poor horse."[49]

While it is not known what Grant, Butler and Foster discussed while Merriam looked on, it may have been the buildup of Union forces at the bridgehead that began within days of this meeting. Grant saw that Foster could not be effective with the small force he had to wield at Deep Bottom. Thus, on July 21, Brigadier General Weitzel had another pontoon bridge thrown up from Jones' Neck to Curle's Neck to support the anticipated reinforcements. Soldiers of the XIX Corps, en route from Louisiana to Washington, were rerouted to Bermuda Hundred to bolster Foster's strength.[50]

Also on July 21, Foster sent the 11th Maine under Lieutenant Colonel John A. Hill to "advance and occupy the enemy's position" at New Market Heights. Moving across to Strawberry Plains, on the south bank of Bailey's Creek, the men advanced to their intended target and began tearing down the works that Graham's men had used to shell the gunboats. In the midst of this destructive orgy, Department of Richmond troops under Martin Gary arrived. A soldier in Company D boasted that "we captured eleven prisoners, but…the enemy appeared in force and caused us to fall back into our intrenchments." The stubborn men returned the next day and then again on the twenty-third, when they finally dug in and spent the night on the ground they had taken. Colonel Leonard D.H. Currie's brigade of the XIX Corps crossed the river and established a line at Tilghman's Gate near the 11ᵗʰ Maine. The *Saugus* and *Mendota* moved up to shell New Market Heights, keeping the Rebels at bay long enough for Hill's men to consolidate their positions. That same day, the second pontoon bridge, referred to as the lower pontoon bridge, was completed.[51]

"WHERE ARE WE TO GET SUFFICIENT TROOPS TO OPPOSE GRANT?"

With the growing bridgehead an ever-expanding threat, Robert E. Lee reached a breaking point on July 23. He decided to send Major General Joseph B. Kershaw's entire division across the river to destroy the pesky bridgehead at Deep Bottom once and for all. He knew that President Jefferson Davis would be uneasy with such a move, so the sage commander sought to assuage his fretful commander in chief:

> *I have thought much upon the subject of intercepting the enemy's communications on [the] James River, and have written to General Ewell that I would spare troops for the purpose if it could be accomplished. I am aware of the difficulties and of the enemy's facilities for cutting off a small force, and our inability to apply a large one. Still I hope something can be obtained…I believe the troops reported to have crossed James River this morning are for the purpose of preventing our operations on the river. I have sent Kershaw's division to Chaffin's Bluff to re-enforce General Conner.*

The stately Lee had grown adept at handling the president's emotions while furtively ensuring that he would obtain his desired outcome.[52] Still, in a letter to his son written the next day, Lee unloaded his own secret worries:

> *I sent yesterday Genl. Kershaw's division to Chaffin's, which I can ill spare & which I fear I shall be obliged soon to recall. Genl Early telegraphs that the 6ᵗʰ and 19ᵗʰ corps, he learned on the 23ʳᵈ, were moving back through Leesburg towards Alexandra. I presume it is for the purpose of returning*

to Grant, when I shall require all the troops I can get. If anything can therefore be done it must be done quickly. I directed Genl Kershaw to take command of the brigades under Conner, examine the enemy's position at Deep Bottom, & see what could be done. I have not heard from him yet… Where are we to get sufficient troops to oppose Grant? He is bringing to him now the 19th Corps, & will bring every man he can get. His talent & strategy consists in accumulating overwhelming numbers.[53]

With his hand forced, Lee sent a dispatch to Lieutenant General Richard H. Anderson at 5:30 a.m., directing that Kershaw's 4,200 men "proceed at once to Chaffin's Bluff, on the north side of the James River." Kershaw was to "let the troops move by a route so as not to be observed by the enemy, and as rapidly as possible without injury to them." The men were marching for Chaffin's Bluff one hour later and had made it to the James River by late afternoon. The men settled into camps east of Chaffin's Bluff at about 6:00 p.m., and Kershaw took over for Ewell after consulting with him at his headquarters.[54]

"Go Home, You Red Devils!"

Very little happened during the day on the twenty-fourth, as Kershaw allowed his men to rest and recuperate after the long, hard march the day before. However, at 8:00 p.m., Kershaw sent a dispatch to Ewell informing him that he was about to do what Lee had sent him here for: attack the enemy. "I shall attack them on the south side of [Bailey's Creek], and if successful will try Deep Bottom," Kershaw stated. Just before midnight, Kershaw sent Henagan's Brigade across Bailey's Creek to threaten the Federal pickets at Tilghman's Gate. The South Carolinians launched a surprise night attack on the picket line of Currie's Brigade. Lieutenant Colonel Paul A. McMichael of the 20th South Carolina bragged to his diary, "[We] drove in the Yankee Pickets, capturing a few and, no doubt, surprised the Yankees no little."

Back at Deep Bottom, Colonel Harris Plaisted of the 11th Maine heard the firing at about 10:30 p.m. and soon discovered that "the position on the New Market and Malvern Hill road [was] lost." Another member of the 11th recalled, "[O]ur brigade was aroused by the firing, and the regiment went into the works on the bluff in anticipation of a general attack." Instead of attacking, however, the gray coats dug in. "Made entrenchments during the night, the men working with bayonets, tin pans, etc. having but four shovels & picks on hand," Lieutenant Colonel McMichael scrawled in his diary.[55]

After a tense night, Foster immediately began to try to reclaim the lost ground since it was vital to Union efforts north of the James. Following an intense barrage from the Rebel artillery, the 11th Maine and Currie's Brigade were tasked with executing this counterattack, but Colonel Plaisted was so disgusted by the previous night's performance by Currie's men that he requested additional help, citing the fact that "these troops could not be relied upon to retake the lost position." Foster concurred and had the 10th Connecticut placed in support. All day long, Foster's skirmishers tentatively pushed forward until they were within sight of their former earthworks. By this point, darkness had begun to fall.[56]

The 3rd South Carolina of Henagan's Brigade had been in reserve during the day's fighting, but all of that was about to change. Lieutenant James "Newt" Martin of Company E recalled that "just about sunset...a curier came dashing up and reported the enemy in our front." The regiment immediately formed into line of battle and pushed a line of skirmishers into the woods to meet Plaisted's oncoming Federals. Martin moved out with his men as the last traces of daylight faded away, advancing some four hundred yards before encountering the Yankees. The skirmishers had stopped briefly to realign their ranks when a voice bellowed from the dark woods in front: "Who comes there?"

According to Martin, "It was answered by about half Doz. muskets." Losing no time, the 3rd broke into a charge, done in the "best style," and easily brushed back the Federals. Some of the men saw that they were fighting men dressed in garish Zouave uniforms with red pantaloons and shouted, "Go home, you red devils!" at their antagonists. The South Carolinians cried out for the fleeing bluecoats to halt, "which some of them obeyed very promptly well," recalled Martin. About twenty prisoners were taken, and upon investigation, it turned out that they belonged to the ill-starred XIX Corps. Martin "injoyed the little frolick very much" and happily learned on the march back to the main line that he hadn't suffered any casualties.[57]

As the twenty-sixth drew to a close, Foster's men had failed to retake their lines at Tilghman's Gate. The 11th Maine lost 1 man killed and 21 men wounded in the attack. As both sides prepared to continue the contest afresh the next morning, they had no idea that a host of 24,500 Federal soldiers was en route to tip the scales in favor of the Union.[58]

"Something in the Way of Offensive Movement"

The mighty Federal host that was on its way to Deep Bottom on the evening of July 26 was sent there as a part of what has come to be known as Grant's Third Offensive of the Richmond-Petersburg Campaign. The genesis of this campaign had its origin in two main factors.

First, Grant was frustrated with the slow progress being made in his investment of Petersburg. Events in Georgia and Maryland were progressing faster than the blundering efforts near the Cockade City, and Grant was being pressured by the Lincoln administration to do something to turn the tide. Out west, Grant's friend Sherman had been attacked by General John Bell Hood at Peachtree Creek, and even though Sherman had achieved a hard-won victory, Grant was concerned that another Confederate effort might be mounted soon. If he did not do something to divert Lee's attention, the Army of Northern Virginia might start sending reinforcements to Hood's army. Furthermore, with Jubal Early's small army roaming around near Washington, D.C., and scoring a victory at Kernstown on July 24, Grant needed to do something to assuage the fears of Abraham Lincoln that another Confederate invasion of the North was forthcoming.

Second, Grant hoped to divert Confederate attention on the Richmond-Petersburg front from an effort that was underway to tunnel underneath the Confederate works at Petersburg and explode a large mine that might lead to the capture of Petersburg and the defeat of Lee's army. This plan had been in the works since June 21, when Lieutenant Colonel Henry Pleasants of the 48th Pennsylvania proposed a plan to use his former coal miners to dig a mine under the Confederate position and blow it sky high. Work began on June 25, and the mine was ready to go by July. Grant hoped an expedition to the north side of the James River would divert Confederate attention away from the mine. As Grant later said, "The mine was constructed and ready to be exploded, and I wanted to take that occasion to carry Petersburg if I could." An attack elsewhere might force Lee to weaken his lines in front of the mine and ensure a Union success in that sector.[59]

With these two factors in mind, Grant wrote in his memoirs, "I concluded then…to do something in the way of offensive movement." The plan that he developed would set the stage for the First Battle of Deep Bottom.[60]

At 8:30 p.m. on the evening of July 25, 1864, Grant sent the instructions for the upcoming Deep Bottom expedition to Major General George G. Meade. A joint force consisting of Major General Winfield Scott Hancock's

II Corps along with two divisions of Sheridan's cavalry and Brigadier General August V. Kautz's Army of the James cavalry division would "make a demonstration on the north side of the James River having for its real object the destruction of the [Virginia Central] Railroad." This combined force would field 24,500 men, and to facilitate a speedy crossing, the infantry was slated to cross the James at the upper pontoon bridge, while the cavalry would cross at the lower pontoon bridge.[61]

The main job of Hancock's infantry was to "advance as rapidly as possible from Deep Bottom until they get opposite Chaffin's Bluff," clearing out any Confederates they encountered along the way. Once this was accomplished, Hancock was to "take up a line to prevent the enemy from throwing a force across the river" and, if possible, "advance towards Richmond...and hold such positions as he may think will insure the greatest security to the expedition." After Chaffin's Bluff had been secured, Phil Sheridan's cavalry troopers were to "advance as rapidly as possible on the Virginia Central Railroad...as near to the city as possible." After destroying all of the bridges over the Chickahominy River, they would "work north as far as the South Anna [River], unless driven off sooner." Once these twin objectives were achieved, "the whole expedition will return and resume their present places."[62]

A conflicted Grant also flirted with the idea of storming into Richmond and seizing the Confederate capital outright. But the general candidly confided to Meade that this idea was "barely possible...The only way it can be done, if done at all, is to ride up to the city boldly...and go in at the first point reached." Grant was speaking out of ignorance, however, for in his haste to get the expedition off he did not reconnoiter the ground or investigate the quantity and quality of the Confederate troops in the vicinity. However, in hindsight, his comments about boldness seem very prescient.[63]

"A FAILURE OF THE EXPEDITION IN THE COMMENCEMENT"

Hancock was informed of his first independent command at 2:30 p.m. on the afternoon of the twenty-fifth when a courier arrived with a note from General Meade containing Grant's original instructions. He immediately issued a circular to his division commanders advising them to keep their men in camp the next day. In the meantime, Hancock got to work marshalling the supplies he would need and requesting everything from an engineer officer to maps and a guide who was familiar with the terrain on the north side of the James.[64]

The corps commander then issued his orders for the march. At 4:00 p.m. on the twenty-sixth, Barlow's First Division was to move out, accompanied by two batteries of artillery and a staff officer who would show him the way. Next came Mott's Third Division, with three batteries, and then Gibbon's Second Division, with two batteries, bringing up the rear. Each division would have twenty ambulances accompany it, with the remainder of the corps ambulances being sent to the supply train. Hancock further made it clear that "no wagons will be allowed to accompany the troops excepting those containing intrenching tools, the headquarters spring wagons, one medical wagon for each division, one wagon for each division for hospital tent[s]…and the necessary transportation for three days' forage." A stern warning was then given that "success will depend to a considerable extent, if not entirely, upon the discipline and steadiness of the troops. Commanders are enjoined to take effective measures to prevent straggling." Finally, should any of the men fall into the hands of the enemy while on the march, they were to give "only their names, and regiments, and no information which will disclose the strength of the command." With these directives disseminated to Hancock's lieutenants, all that could be done now was to wait until the afternoon.[65]

Tuesday the twenty-sixth began as any other mundane day in camp. David Coon of the 36th Wisconsin wrote in his memorandum book that day, "[M]ended my pants; drew rations; boiled some beef. Talk in camp of being a big march on foot." The rumored march became a reality when the men were ordered to start packing up, and they "a little reluctantly and disconsolately saw their camp goods…stowed in close compass and piled into mule drawn wagons…which they should see again—doubtful when." The march to Deep Bottom began on schedule at 4:00 p.m.

By this point in the war, the men of the II Corps were accustomed to the rigors of night marches, and the men plodded forward with little excitement or fanfare. "We knew desperate work lay before us," wrote Major Isaac Hamilton of the 110th Pennsylvania. The first leg of the journey took the men from Petersburg to Point of Rocks on the Appomattox River. A correspondent with the *New York Tribune* accompanied the men and wrote of this portion of the march:

> *It is two miles over a plain stumpy, brambled and encumbered with fallen timber, and then through pine woods by crooked country roads, which is one*

long vista, straight and marched by rows of cedars four miles further; and when beyond that, winding to the left, down a steep hill to the bridge.[66]

Private John Haley, marching with the 17th Maine in Mott's Division, was apparently unaware or unconcerned about Hancock's stern warning against straggling. Finding the pace of the march much too demanding, Haley and some of his comrades, "being too weak to stand such a long and hurried march…decided to refresh ourselves with a little coffee." Ignoring the standing order that said no fires were permitted during a halt, Haley and company quickly had a pot of coffee brewing and were about to enjoy it when members of the hated provost guard—a forerunner of today's military police—rode up and accosted them. Kicking over the coffee and stamping out the fire, the party ordered Haley and his pards to move on quickly.

A disgruntled Haley confided that "I didn't tear myself to pieces to comply," prompting the commander of the guard to shriek, "God damn you. You act like you don't mean to hurry!" According to Haley, "The thermometer of his wrath rose several degrees at my deliberately slow movements, and he drew his cheese knife"—derisive slang for an officer's sword. "He made several threats to decapitate me and then lunged and drove it into my knapsack with such force that I staggered and almost fell," the recalcitrant private reminisced. One of Haley's friends thought that he had been skewered by the provost guard, shouldered his musket and was about to pull the trigger when he realized that his friend had not, in fact, been stabbed. Haley was positive that "my comrade would have scattered the brains of this fellow into the surrounding woods like so much rubbish" had he not quickly shown that he was unharmed. The altercation ended when the provost realized that these stragglers meant business and "put spurs to his animal and departed in haste." Haley made sure to add to his journal account, "*We* moved on at our leisure" (emphasis in original).[67]

The pontoon bridge had been muffled to conceal the sounds of tens of thousands of men, horses and wagons. Once across, small fires lit by Butler's men to illumine the route of march shimmered as far as the eye could see. The correspondent for the *Tribune* described the surreal effect these fires had as the soldiers marched past him:

> [J]ust opposite us is one of the fires that blaze the way, affording light, as they pass, on this side of it, to show us a little of the stream at a time—a dozen soldiers moving in rapid order, coming out of the night and going into the night, and others take their places, and disappear like the first, and so

continually, except [soon] *it may be a few horsemen at the head of a brigade or regiment, and then we hear a clatter of saber scabbards, or perhaps a battery is going by, and we catch in our eyes a sheen of light glancing from the brightness of the guns, but these only briefly for close after either and all is that flow of armed men, like a river passing, still passing, but never passed.*[68]

The cavalry followed soon after, with Sheridan's troopers in the vanguard and Kautz's men bringing up the rear. They were to move by way of Broadway Landing and cross the lower pontoon bridge across the James. During the lengthy ride, some bored cavalry troopers got caught up in a "spirit of reckless mischief" and tossed a few of their cartridges into the fires used to light the way up the Bermuda Hundred Peninsula. The resulting explosions caused some nearby pickets to panic and flee.[69]

General Kautz was packing his belongings and preparing for the upcoming ride when Sheridan stopped by for a brief consultation. As Kautz confided to his diary, "[F]rom him I found that we are not likely to get off until towards morning. I therefore went to bed. The appearance of things indicates a failure of the expedition in the commencement." His division would remain idle until after darkness fell.[70]

At about midnight, Hancock rode past the head of his column to meet with Sheridan and Foster at the latter's headquarters at Deep Bottom. Foster reported to Hancock that the Confederate works in front of his bridgehead were more formidable and better defended than he had originally suspected. As Hancock reported:

The information I derived from conversation with General Foster was briefly as follows: The upper and lower pontoon bridges were above and below Four Mile [Creek], *impassable near its mouth. The enemy held, apparently in considerable force, a strong position near the upper bridge, while their line appeared to terminate nearly opposite the lower bridge.*[71]

With this in mind, Hancock altered the entire plan for the campaign. At 1:30 a.m. on July 27, the anxious general wired to Meade, "From present appearances I judge it would be [a] better plan to cross the lower bridge." He added that "this will...delay Sheridan, but seems the best that can be done under the circumstances." Meade gave Hancock the go-ahead to shift everyone to the lower pontoon, crossing at 2:15 a.m. Hancock notified his subordinates of the change of plan at 3:00 a.m., after many precious hours had wasted away.[72]

The II Corps crossing the James on the evening of July 26. *From* Harper's Weekly.

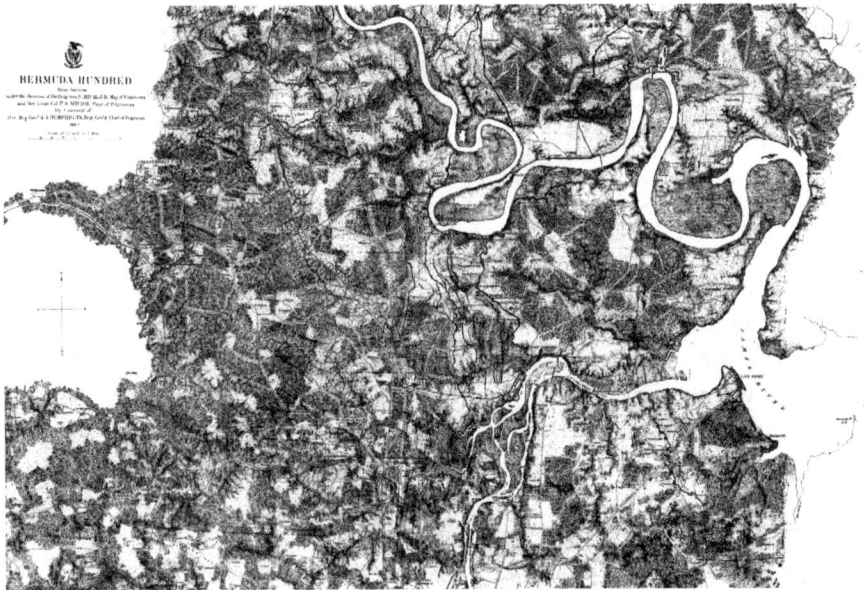

A map of the Bermuda Hundred Peninsula, which Hancock and Sheridan's men traversed on their way to Deep Bottom on July 26. *Courtesy of the Library of Congress.*

The lower pontoon bridge at Deep Bottom. *Courtesy of the Library of Congress.*

This change of plan dealt a deathblow to the entire campaign. Instead of a smoothly conducted crossing of the infantry and cavalry over two separate bridges, Sheridan's troopers were now put on hold and ordered to wait while the entire II Corps crossed the lower bridge before them. Even more egregious was the fact that Hancock had now unwittingly placed himself in a sector more heavily defended than his original crossing point. As Hancock's aide, Francis A. Walker, stated:

> It placed Bailey's Creek between Hancock and his objective point, [Chaffin's] *Bluff. Should the stream be found to afford a good natural line of defense, a force which could not have fought Hancock an hour on the other side of the creek might be enabled to resist him, on this line, long enough to defeat the first purpose of the expedition.*

It appears that Foster's earlier run-ins with Kershaw's men had made him jittery and caused him to overinflate Confederate numbers when he consulted with Hancock.[73]

"THE BLOODY CATTLE HAVE NO MANNERS"

While Hancock was busily fretting and altering his plans for the campaign, the II Corps began crossing the James on the lower pontoon bridge at about 2:00 a.m. The men marched over layers of hay that muffled the sound of their feet. The hay had the desired effect of lessening the noise made by the weary foot soldiers, but a rifleman in the 2nd United States Sharpshooters bemoaned the fact that "the hay was slippery as to make it difficult to keep in the ranks, so that unexpected thumps on the head from rifle barrels were not infrequent." Still, the men trudged on, and the head of the column reached Tilghman's Wharf at about 3:00 a.m. They immediately went into camp and attempted to get some semblance of rest.[74]

When all was said and done, about one-third of the infantrymen in Hancock's command followed the example of John Haley and fell out during the march. Many of them did not rejoin their units until midmorning. Among the very last of the infantry to cross was a feisty Irishman named Paddy Long. The luck of the Irish had apparently run out for Long, who did not reach the James until all of the infantry had passed, and the army butchers were driving a herd of cattle across the bridge. Long attempted to cross but was bumped by one of the cows and sent splashing into the water. Some of Uncle Sam's sailors were kind enough to hop in a small boat and come to Paddy's rescue. He came out sopping wet but intact, and after composing himself, he informed the sailors, "The bloody cattle have no manners." By 8:00 a.m., the infantry had crossed, and now it was finally time for the cavalry to begin crossing.[75]

While the infantry were still crossing the pontoon bridge, Hancock issued a directive that revealed a level of uncertainty about his nascent campaign. In an order to his chief of staff, Colonel Charles H. Morgan, Hancock stated:

> *Let the division commanders be ready at daylight. I shall develop the enemy's position by General Barlow, and, if necessary, by General Mott; seizing, if possible, the position in front and holding the crossing over Four Mile Run. We will then see if we can break through while the cavalry is passing us.*

The timber along Four Mile Creek on your side must be looked after closely. I expect that is strongly held. If General Barlow sees anything at daylight giving him an opportunity let him seize it.

As the sun crept ever higher in the sky, Hancock was already having misgivings about whether or not he should attack.[76]

Chapter 4

Clash at Tilghman's Gate

"A Chill Pervaded the Atmosphere"

With his exhausted troops finally across the James, Hancock wasted little time in attempting to locate the enemy and begin the grand offensive that would open the way for Sheridan to commence his raid. After crossing, the II Corps spread out into an open area called Strawberry Plains, with Barlow's First Division on the left, anchored on Bailey's Creek, and Mott's Third Division on the right. Gibbon's men were held in reserve behind Barlow's Division, while the cavalry troopers began the process of fanning out to the east on Mott's right. As soon as these dispositions were completed, Hancock ordered his brigade commanders to throw out skirmishers and flankers. Observing the calm before the storm, one soldier in the 17th Maine recorded in his journal, "The mists of the morning were just rising and imparted a somber tint to the scene as we formed in line of battle and awaited orders. A chill pervaded the atmosphere, in keeping with the solemnity of the moment."[77]

Just north of the Union expeditionary force were three of Kershaw's brigades, temporarily commanded by Brigadier General Benjamin G. Humphreys. Because of the previous days' fighting with Foster's troops, these Confederates had crossed Bailey's Creek and aligned along the River Road at a place called Tilghman's Gate. From this high ground, they could command any approach from the Deep Bottom bridgehead.

Left: Major General Joseph B. Kershaw. One of Lee's finest division commanders, Kershaw would struggle in independent command north of the James River. *From* Battles and Leaders, *vol. 3.*

Right: Brigadier General Benjamin G. Humphreys commanded the Confederate forces at Tilghman's Gate on July 27, 1864. *Courtesy of the Library of Congress.*

Humphreys's own Mississippi Brigade—consisting of the 13th, 17th, 18th and 21st Mississippi—was east of Bailey's Creek facing south. Graham's Rockbridge Battery was next, "in pits embrazured to fire on the enemy" between Humphreys and Colonel John W. Henagan's South Carolina brigade on the left. Henagan commanded the 2nd, 3rd, 7th, 8th, 15th and 20th South Carolina, along with the 3rd South Carolina Battalion. Gary's 7th South Carolina Cavalry, 24th Virginia Cavalry and Hampton Legion were "about halfway between New Market Heights and Malvern Hill" in supporting distance just beyond Henagan. The Rebels seemed oblivious to the large body of Yankees that had just crossed to the north side, and Kershaw ordered all of the artillery horses to the rear—a decision that would have dire consequences before the day was through.[78]

It just so happened that Tilghman's Gate stood right in Hancock's path, and the corps commander wasted little time in sending out a skirmish line from Barlow's and Mott's Divisions to take the position. Although in reserve, Gibbon assigned the 1st Battalion, Minnesota Infantry, and the 59th, 155th and 170th New York to his skirmish line. At about 6:00 a.m., Barlow pushed forward Brigadier General Nelson A. Miles's 1st Brigade on the left, while Mott deployed his own 1st Brigade, led by Brigadier General Regis de Trobriand. Miles, in turn, tasked Colonel James C. Lynch to take a line of skirmishers, consisting of his own 183rd Pennsylvania and the 28th Massachusetts and 26th Michigan, to advance across the plains. De Trobriand advanced a lengthy skirmish line composed of the 40th New York, 141st Pennsylvania and the 2nd United States Sharpshooters (Berdan's) on the right, as well as the 99th and 110th Pennsylvania on the left, closer to Lynch's troops.[79]

The artillery support for this assault consisted of fourteen cannons led by Major John G. Hazard and the gunboat USS *Mendota*, which was anchored near the lower pontoon bridge at Deep Bottom. For the foot-slogging infantry, the massive one-hundred-pound shells fired by the *Mendota* were a real novelty. A surgeon in the 19th Massachusetts had the good fortune to watch the gunboat in action when he was lounging near the bank of the James:

The USS *Mendota* patrolling the James River near Deep Bottom. *Courtesy of the Library of Congress.*

The crew of the USS *Mendota*. *Courtesy of the National Archives and Records Administration.*

While I write, sitting on the edge of the river, the gunboat Mendota, *a hundred yards off, is throwing hundred-pound shells at* [the enemy] *by signals from on shore and from the mast head, as they cannot see from the deck, and they make some pretty good shots at about three miles. To ride through the woods where they have been shelling it looks as though no living thing could have stayed there.*[80]

The Confederates north of the James had endured this pounding from the cursed Yankee gunboats for weeks now, so they were used to having their breakfasts rudely interrupted. But when the fog lifted, Hazard's guns added their own chorus to the music of the shelling, signaling that Hancock's skirmishers were stepping off. The unsuspecting men of Humphreys's command scrambled pell-mell to meet them.

"MEN, LET A GENERAL LEAD YOU"

The first order of business for De Trobriand's men was to secure the far right flank of the entire Union advance. The 141st Pennsylvania and 2nd U.S. Sharpshooters moved out "without serious opposition to the position assigned to them, around two farmhouses of some importance." Once this was achieved, the remainder of De Trobriand's skirmish line—the 99th and 110th Pennsylvania—continued the advance, moving toward the left to link up with Miles's skirmishers.[81]

While this was taking place, Lynch's skirmish line, under Miles, took aim for the right flank of the Confederate line. As the men advanced, they came closer and closer to the 10th Connecticut and 11th Maine of Foster's command, who were still holding a line of rifle pits west of Tilghman's Gate. Major Henry Camp of the 10th Connecticut watched in awed amazement the spectacle that unfolded before his eyes as Lynch's men plodded on, each step taking them closer within range of the Confederate line:

We watched them with intent eagerness. As they rose to the level beyond, a sharp volley greeted them; and instantly the air was white and the hillside dotted with puffs of smoke as each man halted for an instant where he stood, fired, and moved on loading for another discharge. There is one poor fellow down! and an officer, a surgeon perhaps, bending over him. There are half a dozen more!—not all of them wounded, however: they are lying flat for cover, and we can see them loading and firing industriously. There are two or three mounted officers—one of them with a straw hat—cantering about among the men.[82]

In spite of all the bravery that Lynch (the officer in the straw hat) could muster, his men would not withstand the volume of the Rebel musketry. They fell back behind hilly ground and lay down. John Ryan of the 28th Massachusetts recalled, "We had orders to 'double quick.' In the meantime our batteries were firing on the Confederates and the shots passed over our heads. We advanced as far as the foot of [a] hill and laid down." One officer observed disdainfully that "our men struggled badly," and for the moment, the Confederates were safe.[83]

Knowing that his men could not stay in the position they currently held, Lynch rallied his men for a second attempt at taking the works. Once again, Major Camp had a front-row seat for the action:

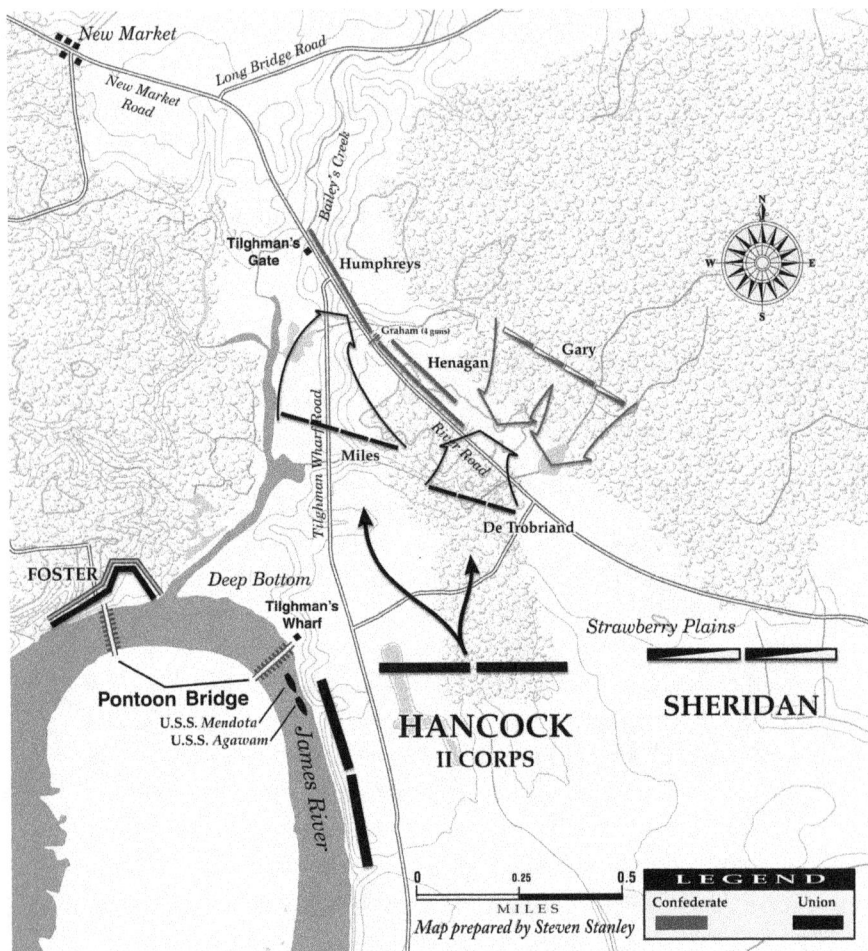

The fighting near Tilghman's Gate, July 27, 1864. *Map by Steven Stanley.*

[Lynch] *gallops to and fro, waving his sword, pointing to the front, pressing them to come up once more. Some are ready to try it. The color-bearer rushes forward, stands on the highest point of ground where the bullets must be flying like hail, turns and waves his colors to those behind. We can hardly help cheering the brave fellow, and that noble rider who is in front of all, dashing on, and calling them to follow. We expect every moment to see him go down, and strain our eyes with eager watching. How can men help following him?*[84]

In a matter of minutes, Lynch's second attempt had failed.

By now, however, De Trobriand's men were in close supporting distance. As they continued their link-up with Lynch's beleaguered skirmishers, an officer in the 110th Pennsylvania spotted Graham's Battery and began moving in that direction, sidling in east of Lynch's right flank. As De Trobriand later recalled:

> *The One Hundred and Tenth which connected on the left with the other brigade, observed four guns in position within a short distance. Their fire was immediately turned obliquely on the artillerymen, while the Ninety Ninth and the Seventy Third, continuing to engage the infantry, obliqued toward the left to draw nearer the cannon.*[85]

When Henagan's South Carolinians observed the 110th zeroing in on Graham's Battery, they immediately moved to meet them. Humphreys had also seen the threat and called for the artillery horses, only then realizing that Kershaw had sent them to the rear. A courier from Gary arrived at the same time to give him the unwelcome news that he already knew too well: he was flanked. Humphreys sent word back to Gary that he was to attack immediately. Graham's Battery now moved its guns into the road and pointed them toward the Pennsylvanians, now about fifty yards away. Once in the road, the battery could only bring two guns to bear on the Yankee menace. Unfazed by this disadvantage, the experienced gunners fired several rounds of canister, which halted the 110th, and they also lobbed enough shells at Lynch's men to discourage them from keeping up the attack.[86]

While all of this was taking place, the *Mendota* continued to fire its colossal shells. One of Henagan's men observed with horror as "the Gun Boats throwed Several 2 hundred Pounders over amongst us [and]...a shell struck our orderly Sergt. in the Breast Bursting at the same time tearing him literly to pieces the poor fellow never knew what struck him."[87]

With Graham's guns now deployed in the road, Henagan responded in turn by adjusting his right wing to meet the threat posed by De Trobriand. One Rebel noted that this maneuver "was so badly performed as to partake very much of the nature of a retreat." As they attempted to come on line beside Graham, "their right, instead of resting on the battery, was from twenty to fifty yards in the rear of it." Another Confederate lamented that Henagan now had "part of the line resting on the road and the rest bearing off at an obtuse angle into the woods." This hindered rather than helped the

Left: Brigadier General Regis de Trobriand. *Courtesy of the Library of Congress.*

Right: Brigadier General Nelson Miles. *Courtesy of the Library of Congress.*

plight of Humphreys's line, and it was evident that the position could not hold out for much longer.[88]

The last glimmer of hope had indeed already faded, for when Henagan executed his botched maneuver to come to the assistance of Graham's Battery, he created a fifty-yard gap in Humphreys's overall line. This was almost directly across from where Lynch's skirmish line continued its onslaught. With Lynch drawing near to their position, the men of the 10th Connecticut and 11th Maine deemed the time propitious to get into the fight, and they "opened an effective fire upon the enemy." Lynch's men took refuge behind some rolling ground, and the colonel took this opportunity to plant his colors and re-form his tattered line. At this point, Miles himself rode up and inspired his troops by bellowing, "Men, let a general lead you." The 28th Massachusetts now conducted a left half wheel to bring it to bear squarely against Henagan's left, leaving precious few grains of sand in the Confederate hourglass.[89]

"IT WAS MADNESS TO ATTEMPT TO HOLD OUT"

Hazard's field pieces continued to shellac Humphreys's beleaguered troops, making it nearly impossible for them to mount an effective resistance. A member of Battery B, 1st Rhode Island Light Artillery, later bragged that his gunners "by a careful and well directed fire, landed our shot in the midst of the rebel battery, making it rather uncomfortable for them and their position untenable." This vicious combination forced Humphreys into deciding that he must retreat. As Humphreys explained to Kershaw a few days later:

> *Gen. Gary did not attack in time. When the enemy advanced, the parrot guns opened fire upon the line. This drew upon them and the two regiments, the fire of the skirmish line in front, and the artillery from the Tete Du Pont which perfectly enfiladed them. The infantry supports gave way.*[90]

In the fog of war, the word to retreat did not filter down to the gunners of Graham's Battery, who were busy loading and discharging their massive guns as quickly as they could. They remained preoccupied with this task until Lynch's skirmishers were within fifty yards. A soldier in the 5th New Hampshire stated that his fellow skirmishers "made big demonstrations in front as tho we were going to charge directly on them & drew all their fire on us. [W]hile the line on our right swung around their left & took them in rear." At this point, Graham's cannoneers attempted to withdraw their guns, but the fire of the 11th Maine and 10th Connecticut prevented the artillerymen from bringing off the Parrott rifles. The artillerymen, in the words of Private James Rawlings, had to "abandon the guns and run for it," barely escaping capture. One of Graham's gunners later offered a defense of his actions to a Richmond newspaper:

> *Our supply of canister, being small, as is always the case with heavy rifled guns, had run short, but the guns were turned to the right again and fired shell until the enemy were within 50 yards. Our infantry, in the meantime, did not fire a shot, and seeing that it was madness to attempt to hold out, we abandoned our pieces and sought the cover of the woods.*

A fellow artillerist with the Richmond Howitzers watched the retreat of Graham's gunners and stated that "no blame can be attached to the men or to the Captain of that brave company, whose brilliant name was won on fields where 'Stonewall' Jackson fought and conquered."[91]

The capture of Graham's Battery, as depicted by William Waud. The sketch contains a handwritten note: "[S]ee daily papers this is called the fight at Strawberry Plains. When our men charged the Gunners fled through the woods taking their Sponge staffs with them." *Courtesy of the Library of Congress.*

With the cannoneers fleeing, Lynch's men surged into the Confederate position at Tilghman's Gate. The men of the 10th Connecticut and 11th Maine rushed forward to join their comrades from the Army of the Potomac. One soldier in the 28th Massachusetts noted wryly that "the Confederates left the entrenchments pretty lively," while another soldier jotted in his diary that the Rebs scattered "in precipitate flight." The Yankee went on to say that "the skirmishers might have saved themselves, but instead tried to save the guns. They failed to do either." A correspondent for the *New York Herald* scrutinized an exhausted Colonel Lynch, whom he described as "uninjured, although two bullets passed through his hat and another hit his horse."[92]

Lynch was happy to see that his men captured all four of Graham's Parrott rifles, along with their caissons and ammunition chests. On an ironic note, it was discovered that all of these guns had once belonged to the Union—one was taken by "Stonewall" Jackson's men at Harper's Ferry before the Battle of Antietam, and the other three were captured by Ewell's troops during the Gettysburg Campaign. Artillerymen from the 10th Massachusetts Battery triumphantly hitched up the guns and hauled them off.[93]

Humphreys pulled back across Bailey's Creek and took shelter in an unfinished portion of the New Market Line. The Mississippian overlooked the situation and "made no attempt to retake but immediately gave orders for the withdrawal of all my command to the trenches at Darbytown Road and New Market Heights." Left with little to boast about, he told Kershaw that this passage "was effected without loss."[94]

When he reached safety, an irate Captain Graham asked for muskets "that his men might rally around him and retake the guns," but by then it was too late. The talented young artillerist blamed Henagan's men, whom he said "gave way without making an effort to save the guns."[95]

Incredibly, from the opening shot to the time that Lynch's skirmish line took the Confederate earthworks, the action at Tilghman's Gate lasted only fifteen minutes. Humphreys reported that his command lost a total of fifty-one men—seven men killed, thirty-seven wounded and seven missing. The attacking Federals lost ninety-five men, of whom seventeen were fatalities. The Federal expedition had gotten off to a great start, prompting one Yankee private to jot down in his journal, "[T]his was an excellent beginning for us."[96]

"ONE OF THE BRAVEST ACTS OF THE WAR"

An excellent start it may have been, but the fighting at Tilghman's Gate was not quite over just yet. In a bizarre postscript, Brigadier General Martin Gary's brigade arrived on the scene shortly after the Federal forces triumphed, responding to Humphreys's earlier order to attack. Just as the Federals were planning to follow up on the River Road, Gary threw caution to the wind and decided to attack. One of his men recalled how "[w]e rode some five miles, were dismounted and sent to the front." The Bald Eagle sallied forth with everything he had on hand—the Hampton Legion, 7th South Carolina, 24th Virginia and a battery of twelve-pound cannons. It would be six hundred men versus the gathering might of the entire II Corps.[97]

In "one of the bravest acts of the war," Gary posted the 24th Virginia and his cannons in support and sent in the Hampton Legion and 7th South Carolina, both of which quickly threw out a skirmish line in a cornfield while the cannons opened up on De Trobriand's men.[98]

Charles Crosland of Gary's command described the terrain:

In our rear was a heavy growth of oak timber, and in our front a large field of corn about seven feet high, just in the bunch to tassel. It was very thick and the enemy were there in large numbers. We lay in a little ditch about a foot and a half deep, its bank being thrown up and a low plank fence put upon it.[99]

Battery B, 1st Rhode Island Light Artillery, and two guns of Sleeper's 10th Massachusetts Battery began to trade shots with Gary's cannoneers. De Trobriand also ordered the 141st Pennsylvania to throw out a line of skirmishers, while the 99th and 110th Pennsylvania marched into the cornfield to flush out the pesky Confederates. The boys of Battery B managed to score a direct hit on a Confederate caisson, causing the gunners to fly in panic, and the *Mendota* zeroed in on the cornfield, prompting Crosland to remember how

the fire from their gunboats and field artillery was fearful, the shells hissing, shrieking and bursting all around us, tearing off whole tree tops and limbs in our rear; the grape and cannister making a fearful rattling and sickening thud, striking tree trunks, was very demoralizing. They were so thick it sounded like…lightning and hail striking many times a minute.[100]

Lieutenant Colonel Casper W. Tyler of the 141st Pennsylvania "directed four companies to be deployed and advanced them about 100 yards into an intervening corn-field," where they began to trade shots with the enemy. In the meantime, the 99th and 110th Pennsylvania had just entered the cornfield, where they were received by a staggering volley from the woods in front of them. De Trobriand witnessed the intensity of the Rebel fire and sent the 73rd New York to reinforce the struggling Pennsylvanians. Gary's men were desperate to hold on, with one trooper recalling that "as fast as we fired we laid down in the ditch to reload, and up and fired again." The two sides stood their ground, trading shots with a cool intensity, determined to win the day.[101]

One company of the Hampton Legion under the command of Captain Ben Nicholson went so far as to launch a ferocious counterthrust, which caused De Trobriand's men to falter momentarily. Gary later described how Nicholson "gallantly led his company…until he reached within easy pistol range. He fired upon them, causing the enemy's Regiment to withdraw in great disorder." After capturing several prisoners, Nicholson "threw his company perpendicular to the [River] road, thereby protecting the flank of the regiment." While Nicholson's men formed perpendicular to the road, the other men of the Legion used the bank of the River Road as protection and opened a blistering fire on the Yankees. William T. Walton recalled:

> *Our company was sent out in a clear place to check the Yankees so the command could cross this swamp. We went to this place, the Yankees coming through a straw field, in a solid line of infantry, and when we got there the Yankees were about 150 yards coming on. We shot at them. I aimed at the colors and they fell, but others shot at them too. We fell down on our backs to load again, and to let their balls pass over us. When I got my gun loaded, I got up to shoot and could see only one Yankee running half bent toward a hollow. I shot at him and he fell. At this time we were nearly cut off, so we went to the swamp of timber to cross over. The Yankees' balls were knocking the bark off the logs, as they came at us. The man behind me said for me to go faster, but I told him I could not, I had no one to be dodging behind. One can imagine what it meant to be dodging balls that even knocked bark off the logs one walked on. I was so spent when I got across that I fell, but got to the breastworks unhurt.[102]*

Sixteen-year-old C.M. Maull of Company G, Hampton Legion, was serving as a courier for Martin Gary when he had a more harrowing experience. While carrying a message to Colonel Thomas M. Logan, a bullet whizzed past his ears. He described what happened next:

> *I looked over to the left and perceived about one hundred yards from me a blue coat partly hid behind one of the larger trees, in the act of taking a cartridge from his cartridge box to reload his rifle. I stuck spurs to my horse and dashed up to the tree thinking I would compel him to surrender, his gun being empty, but when I arrived there he met me at the point of his bayonet. Keeping the tree between us, I had drawn my saber when I started toward him and had it now uplifted to cut him down. He was a very large German, weighing about one hundred and eighty pounds, I would suppose. I called on him to surrender. He said something in German consigning me in all probability to a warm place. I found myself in a fix. I knew that if I rode off I would be shot ere I could get out of reach of his bullet so making the best of a bad bargain I rode around the tree in hopes of getting a cut with my saber, but as I would ride around he would get on the other side, keeping the tree between him and myself. We played go round the merry gold bush for about a half hour when he became tired of the sport, I suppose,*

and stepped from behind the tree and made a vicious lunge at me with his bayonet. I had my eye on him and was prepared for him. As he stepped from the shelter of the tree I made a down cut with my saber simultaneous with his lunge, cleaving through his cap and partly through his skull. His bayonet passed through my right leg a little above the knee cap, the saddle tree about an inch or more in the side of my horse's back and he in falling, held on to his rifle in a death grip, the bayonet breaking just above the socket leaving me pinned to my saddle and no means of extracting myself. I studied awhile and in a few moments made up my mind the best thing I could do was to turn back and make tracks for the regimental hospital, hoping to meet another courier and turn my dispatch over to him which I fortunately did. [103]

In spite of the individual feats of bravery by Walton, Maull and others, Gary's Confederates were simply overwhelmed by the sheer number of Federal troops De Trobriand was throwing at them. Further, in a bizarre replay of what had happened only moments earlier with Graham's Battery, De Trobriand's bluecoats focused on the twelve-pounders that Gary had brought with him. They, too, it seemed, wished to share in the glory of capturing a few of the enemy's guns. When the Union troops surged toward the cannons, six whole companies of Major John R. Robertson's 24th Virginia Cavalry broke, the major himself running pell-mell for safety.[104]

General Gary rode up to the men of the 7th South Carolina Cavalry and ordered them to charge down the road and retake the line, but the men balked. Crosland recalled how Gary "took out his pistols and threatened to shoot us if we did not move on. He ranted and fumed, but the men were dogged and remained firm." One target of Gary's ire was a certain Captain Tucker, to whom Gary gave "'Hail Columbia' with many oaths, delivered with great emphasis."[105]

In an amusing incident directly following the fighting, Captain Tucker approached Gary and expressed his hurt feelings at being verbally abused

Brigadier General Martin Gary. *From Miller's* Photographic History of the Civil War.

in front of his men. Tucker also added, "I wish to know why you cursed me a while ago, on the skirmish line." Gary explained that it was a bad habit that he had developed and consoled the officer by telling him, "[N]ext time I curse you, you just curse me back, and I will take no offense."

Tucker haughtily explained to the general that he was not the cursing sort, at which point Gary bluntly ended the exchange by stating, "Then, I don't know what in the hell you will do."[106]

While Captain Tucker was busy dodging Yankee bullets and Gary's epithets, Captain Theophilus Barham took the four remaining companies of the 24th Virginia to defend the cannons until they could be limbered up and taken off the field. Barham was credited with saving the guns, but the sheepish officer later revealed that "my opinion is the credit was accidental, but accidents sometimes happened in the army." Regardless, a second disaster was staved off, and Gary could give the signal for his men to retreat. He had lost fourteen casualties in this forlorn hope.[107]

"ALL CHANCES FOR SURPRISING THE ENEMY HAD PASSED"

While the action at Tilghman's Gate was raging, Sheridan joined Hancock at his headquarters near the lower pontoon bridge, and the two flamboyant officers smoked cigars and appreciated the doting gazes of their men. One such gawker later recalled how "both [Hancock and Sheridan] sat their horses as only perfect horsemen and hard riders can, and both puffed away at cigars, and both seemed as flattered as amused by the admiring glances... of our men."[108] One visitor who was not so spellbound was Lieutenant Colonel Cyrus B. Comstock of Grant's staff.

At about 7:00 a.m., Comstock rode up and talked with the two smoking chieftains. The stiff resistance put up by Humphreys and Gary had rattled Hancock, who was unsure how to proceed now that the element of surprise had been lost. Comstock was amazed to learn that both Hancock and Sheridan "seemed to think...the thing was a failure," and rather than pressing forward, they asked Comstock to ride back to City Point and consult with Grant as to what they should do next. Comstock had none of it and "told Hancock there was no question that Gen. Grant wished [the] enemy driven into Chaffin's Farm & [Grant] gave orders to push on." Nonetheless, an order was an order, and a perplexed Comstock left

Deep Bottom and rode back to Grant. That evening, Comstock wrote in his diary his opinion that "nothing...was effected owing to the excessive fear of such a disaster as that which happened to the 2nd and 6th Corps in trying to get on the Weldon RR."[109]

While Confederate cannons were still within range, Horace Porter of Grant's staff also paid Hancock a visit. The jittery Porter threw himself on the ground as soon as a fresh salvo of shells whizzed past. During a lull in the firing, Porter apparently informed Hancock that Grant intended to pay a visit later in the day. When shells began falling around them, the small party of officers jumped up and ran to mount their horses. Porter bumped up against Hancock and was responsible for a slight wound to Hancock's personal attire. As Porter recounted the tale:

> *Hancock wore a thin blue flannel blouse, and as I rose up one of my spurs caught in the sleeve, and ripped it open from wrist to elbow. I felt not a little chagrined to find that I was the means of sending this usually well-dressed corps commander into battle with his sleeve slit open and dangling in the air, and made profuse apologies. There was not much time for words, but Hancock treated the matter so good-naturedly in what he said in reply that he at once put my mind at ease.*[110]

Shortly after Comstock's and Porter's visits, Hancock decided that his three divisions would pursue the Confederates now entrenched near Bailey's Creek, but in order to accomplish this, he would have to reorient his corps from facing north to facing west. He thus ordered a left wheel to bring the corps to the east side of Bailey's Creek facing west, with Gibbon's Division anchoring the left, Barlow in the center and Mott still on the right. Maneuvering an entire corps was a painstaking and lengthy process for the volunteer armies of the American Civil War, and this movement ate up much of the morning.

These complicated movements were set into motion in order to clear the way for Sheridan's cavalrymen to dart to the north and begin their raid against the railroad, but at 7:25 a.m., Hancock sent a dispatch to General Andrew Humphreys, the army's chief of staff, to inquire whether they should even bother. Confessing that "all chances for surprising the enemy had passed," Hancock inquired whether "Sheridan's cavalry should attempt to break through the enemy's lines for the purpose of making a raid as had been contemplated, or whether the cavalry should wait until the infantry advanced farther." Hancock's timidity allowed

Humphreys's men to improve their shallow earthworks and turn them into a formidable impediment.[111]

While the Rebels who had been pushed back from Tilghman's Gate frantically dug in, all the while taking fire from the *Mendota* and II Corps batteries, Kershaw—who had just arrived on the scene—saw that he had to have artillery support if he was to maintain his current position. He thus sent a request to Ewell for a few batteries, commanded by Lieutenant Colonel John C. Pemberton, of Vicksburg fame. Telling the South Carolinian that "you will have to look mainly to the troops under your own command to defend the approaches to Richmond," Ewell took care of his own needs at Chaffin's Bluff and seemed content to give Kershaw advice on how he should make his dispositions. The sector between Chaffin's Bluff and New Market Heights was guarded by three units from Ewell's department—the 25th Virginia Battalion, Major Alexander Stark's Light Artillery Battalion and two batteries of Lieutenant Colonel Charles E. Lightfoot's Artillery Battalion—and it appears that one of Kershaw's subordinates "refused to let Lightfoot leave…and placed Stark's battalion nearby." With this divided command structure hampering the Confederates, the timidity of Hancock was a godsend.[112]

At 10:00 a.m., Ewell sent word to Adjutant General Samuel Cooper, explaining that "it may be advisable to send the Local Defense troops to Chaffin's farm to hold the intrenched camp." The hapless Pemberton joined with Ewell, stating that he "deem[ed] it strongly advisable" for the local defense troops to be sent to Chaffin's Bluff to free the rest of the troops there, to parry the next thrust from the meddlesome Yankee invaders. When Confederate secretary of war James A. Seddon caught wind of this, he immediately sought to prevent it. Reasoning that it would disrupt the function of the Confederate administration since so many of the men were government employees, an agitated Seddon wrote to Lee and explained that "such embarrassment results from calling out the local troops that the President prefers the call should not be made till further advices or greater appearance of danger." The word must have spread through the government offices, as War Department clerk John Jones scribbled in his diary, "The clerks are ordered out this afternoon at five, to march to Chaffin's Farm." Ewell's refusal to reinforce Kershaw, coupled with his desire for the local defense troops to bolster his defenses, seems to indicate that he was hunkering down, determined to give a good performance that might reestablish his reputation.[113]

The tumult in the Rebel high command caused a paralysis that— if Hancock had decided to be aggressive—could have resulted in the

Confederates being pushed out of the Bailey's Creek line and forced much closer to Richmond. But Hancock was content to sit on his hands, wait for the cavalry to move out to his right and explore the possibilities for flanking the Confederate line. This lull prompted Grant to personally investigate why his orders to press the attack were not being followed. At 8:25 p.m., Meade received a terse note from the general in chief: "In one hour I shall start for Deep Bottom. Dispatches addressed to me there will reach me."[114]

Chapter 5

Confidence Lost

"Don't Lose Your Bridges"

While the fighting at Tilghman's Gate was taking place, Foster was involved in fighting of his own north of the upper pontoon bridge. At 7:20 a.m., Foster sent word to the Army of the James that "the enemy appear to have fallen back. I am about to make a demonstration on this side to attract attention." Consequently, at 8:00 a.m., the 100th New York and 24th Massachusetts, supported by the 11th Maine and a section of the 1st Connecticut Light Battery, made a demonstration toward the home of Alfred R. Buffin on the New Market Line. Two hours later, Foster sent an update to Brigadier General Godfrey Weitzel, stating, "I am pushing my line near the [Buffin] house and shall try and drive the enemy into their intrenchments," to which Weitzel curtly replied, "All right. Go in, but don't lose your bridges by it." With that note of encouragement, Foster forged ahead.[115]

Facing Foster's men were a small contingent of the 23rd Tennessee and Lane's North Carolina Brigade under the command of Colonel John D. Barry. Barry, only twenty-five years old, was a troubled soul still trying to overcome the night of May 2, 1863, when he personally ordered his skirmishers to fire on "Stonewall" Jackson and his entourage even after he was alerted to the fact that he was firing on his own men. Lane, who had been wounded at Cold Harbor the previous month, was recuperating at the home of Dr. Otis F. Manson near the battlefield. When Barry went down with a wound that morning, he, too, was sent to the physician's home for treatment. Foster's skirmishers pushed all the way to the Buffin House but retired that afternoon when the fighting stopped. Command of Lane's North Carolinians fell to Colonel Robert Van Buren Cowan.[116]

Back at Tilghman's Gate, Gibbon and Barlow began to tentatively push forward out of their newly captured earthworks. At about 9:30 a.m., Gibbon began to probe west toward Bailey's Creek. He once again pulled regiments from each of his brigades to form his skirmish line. Captain James C. Farwell of the 1st Minnesota Battalion remembered that "[w]e…advanced to the woods in our front, when I received orders from Colonel Pierce…to deploy my battalion as skirmishers, my right resting on Four-Mile Creek. This I accomplished without loss, although exposed to the fire of their skirmishers, who were concealed behind trees." Major John Byrne's 155th New York advanced alongside the Minnesotans, who advanced one mile before finding the Confederates "strongly posted and fortified in a commanding position."[117]

Colonel John D. Barry commanded Lane's Brigade until he was wounded on July 27, 1864. *Courtesy of the Library of Congress.*

At 9:15 a.m., Hancock's staff officer Francis Walker updated Barlow on the situation and informed him of his open-ended plan:

> *General Gibbon has already ordered his skirmish line advanced, and has just sent to see that it is done. General Mott will be at once ordered to connect his skirmishers with your right, though refusing his own until the cavalry is in position. The major-general commanding does not desire any advance but a temporary one, with a view to ascertaining the enemy's position. Vedettes can be pushed forward cautiously.*[118]

Hancock was determined to have every detail attended to before he launched another attack. By 10:30 a.m., Gibbon's men were ready to attack across Bailey's Creek, but the fretful Hancock would not let the attack take place until all of the supporting artillery was in place. "Owing to the difficulty of our planting artillery, some delay took place in posting our guns and following up the temporary success we had obtained." Major Hazard explained that "[n]o other positions practicable for artillery could be found on the line."[119]

Precious minutes ticked away, and still no word for the attack was given. While Gibbon's men were idle, Barlow's soldiers pressed forward into the slash at 11:00 a.m. to keep probing the Confederate works along Bailey's Creek. "Barlow made a vigorous reconnaissance," recalled Lieutenant Colonel Walker, "but did not succeed in finding the extreme flank of the enemy, who, by his time, had been largely reinforced." Still, the fighting was intense enough for a member of the 28th Massachusetts to recall, "We had some pretty lively skirmishing in the woods with them." If the fighting continued to develop, Gibbon's support would be needed.[120]

More than four hours after Gibbon had moved out from his recently captured works, eight cannons had been placed close enough to support an attack; Gibbon was ready to move. Hancock joined Gibbon after informing Foster around 12:15 p.m. that the long-awaited attack was finally about to take place. For a few moments, the old Hancock of Williamsburg and Cemetery Ridge was back, and the prospect of action reinvigorated the weary corps commander. Then his eyes examined the newly erected works across Bailey's Creek. As Hancock later explained:

> Bailey's Creek is so much of an obstacle that a line of battle could not well cross it under fire, and the distance from the creek to works was about 1,000 yards, the intervening ground being perfectly open. The works appeared to be filled with men, and a number of pieces of artillery were in position. After a careful examination of the position it was decided that the chances of successful assault were unfavorable, and it was determined to maneuver to the right, with the view of turning the position.[121]

By noon, Sheridan and Kautz's cavalry contingent had finally finished crossing the James. Hancock decided to use the newly arrived horsemen to scout to the right of Barlow and probe for the Confederate flank. With this request, Hancock completely abolished the original plan of attack—instead of sending the cavalry out on an independent raid, they were now to be utilized as close infantry support and scouts. First, Sheridan sent several parties out to scout the roads. Sheridan tasked Brigadier General Alfred Torbert's 1st Cavalry Division with this particular mission. Torbert sent the 6th New York Cavalry from Colonel Thomas C. Devin's Brigade

Brigadier General Alfred T.A. Torbert. *Courtesy of the Library of Congress.*

in the direction of Malvern Hill. Elements of Brigadier General Wesley Merritt's Reserve Brigade were pushed out in the direction of the Long Bridge Road.

In the meantime, Barlow's lethargic skirmish line did not reach Bailey's Creek until well into the afternoon. Barlow now began to probe for a chink in the Confederate armor. The fact that Barlow took so long may have caused Hancock to grow overly concerned, for two brigades of Mott's Division were sent to bolster the youthful general's lines. Mott was pleased when this was accomplished with "very little resistance." From all indications, the Union effort was well into the process of unraveling, with precious minutes of daylight burning away and no sense of urgency on display. Someone needed to take charge of this vast operation before it was too late. Luckily, Ulysses S. Grant arrived at Hancock's headquarters at 1:00 p.m.[122]

"I Shall Be as Cautious as Possible to Avoid Any Bad Luck"

By this point, Grant had been led to believe that Hancock was losing control of the situation. When he and his entourage arrived at corps headquarters at the lower pontoon bridge and no one was there to greet him, he may have taken that as a sign that Hancock was finally heeding his orders to push his infantry forward so Sheridan's raid could begin. The lieutenant general rode around the Deep Bottom front for two hours, no doubt consuming several cigars as his attempts to locate and confer with Hancock proved fruitless. When they arrived, Grant inquired, "Where is the general?"

"Out on the line," came the reply.

"Any telegrams for me?" he then asked.

"No, sir—wire down."

Turning to General Rufus Ingalls, Grant stated, "Rufus, we must see the front, come."[123]

The party rode to visit General Foster at the Grover House, where a staff officer who accompanied him watched as they sat on the front porch and "commented on the good shots the artillery was making." While Grant did not see what the corps commander was up to, he was able to observe that the Confederates were improving their works and that if the attack wasn't pushed forward soon, the entire expedition would be a wash. Indeed, the fact that Sheridan had not even begun his raid was telling.

At 3:30 p.m., Grant returned to Foster's headquarters at Deep Bottom and sent Hancock a message:

> *In looking at the situation, I do not see that much is likely now to be done. If, however, you can push past the enemy's flank and double him back on Chaffin's Bluff, so as to let the cavalry out to perform their part of the expedition, do so. If you do not find this practicable, remain on the north side of the James until you receive further orders. There has been no further movement of troops from the south side of the river to interfere with you. All there is in your front is supposed to be seven brigades with a small force of cavalry. I will now return to headquarters. Please direct your dispatches to be duplicated, one going to men and one going to General Meade.*[124]

At 4:00 p.m., ten minutes after he received Grant's note, Hancock was quick to explain that he had not snubbed the general but had "waited at the front, where I was told you were coming." He reassured Grant that "I shall be as cautious as possible to avoid any bad luck" and explained that he currently had troops who were probing for the Confederate left. The language of aggressive action was nowhere to be found in this strange litany of excuses. Hancock said things like, "I will try and carry out your views, but doubt whether anything can be done," and explained that "the troops are very tired" and "I would have accomplished more except for the weariness of my command." That Hancock blamed his failure to complete the mission on his own men was telling.[125]

"The Sight Is None the Less Exciting"

Hancock's lack of urgency must have been infectious, for Sheridan displayed no great hurry in pushing his scouts forward. They trotted along at a jaunty pace. Torbert's division did not complete the ride up the Long Bridge Road until nearly 5:00 p.m., four hours after it set out. Merritt's Reserve Brigade encountered some of Gary's men in a strong skirmish line protecting the road near the Darby House. The 2nd U.S. Cavalry—one of the oldest cavalry units in the U.S. Army that included among its former officers Confederate lieutenant general Richard H. Anderson—was in the lead. Sheridan observed this fabled unit charge, gratified to watch as the Rebels "were soon driven in on their main line, and the high ground before the house was immediately occupied by Torbert." A newspaper correspondent with the *New York Tribune* also observed this charge and attempted to describe it to his readers:

> *Now an actual cavalry charge is not the ideal cavalry charge. The riders do not go all abreast in a serried phalanx. They go in all a scamper according to the speed of their horses, and the daring of their riders—two variable quantities that scatter the cavalrymen like so many stampeded wild horses. But the sight is none the less exciting and some of us do not repress a cheer or two. The enemy, although 300 strong, do not stand, and we have a dozen prisoners.*[126]

Casualties in this affair were light, and Gary's men fell back to Fussell's Mill, where they ended their momentous day of fighting. After the action, Sheridan sent word to Hancock:

> *The First U.S. Cavalry advanced down the road and met your picket-line on the Long Bridge and New Market road, and made connection. The Second U.S. Cavalry and First New York...are following up the enemy to the left and rear of their infantry line in the direction of Richmond.*[127]

This skirmish alerted Hancock to the fact that the Confederates occupied the Darbytown and Charles City Roads and that Sheridan could not use those roads to launch his raid on the railroad. With his update sent to Hancock, Sheridan now ordered his horse soldiers to bed down for the night. Torbert's Division set up camp on the grounds of the Darby Farm, where they spent a quiet evening.

At 6:00 p.m., Hancock sent word to Meade that he had not succeeded in his great turning movement and that Sheridan could advance no farther up Darbytown Road. "Wherever I struck the enemy's line I found his infantry," the dispirited general reported. Making matters worse, it appeared that the only way left open for Sheridan's troopers to launch their raid was via Bottoms Bridge to the northeast. Sheridan had made this plain when he advised, "If I am to go on I can go on the Long Bridge road and cross the Chickahominy at Bottom's Bridge."[128]

Meade asked Grant to consider this plan. With the Chickahominy at his back, Sheridan and Kautz would be compelled to rejoin the army at Fortress Monroe once the raid was complete. Grant had learned over the past two months that he could not afford to have his cavalry commander detached from the main force for too long, and thus he decided against this course of action. Grant concluded his response optimistically, avowing that "[i]t looks to me as if the cavalry might move well out and get in rear of the enemy." Meade forwarded Grant's orders not to send Sheridan via Bottoms Bridge and ordered Hancock to "be governed by them accordingly." Meade also included a sliver of good news: "I have suggested to the lieutenant-general… that you be re-enforced by any troops General Butler may have to spare." Meade was able to secure 2,600 reinforcements to Hancock in the form of Brigadier General Henry W. Birge's Brigade of the XIX Corps. Butler was reluctant to let these men go, warning, "I do not know how to spare them in case of attack," but they were nonetheless forwarded north of the James. With Birge's reinforcements holding the line, Hancock could throw all of the II Corps into the turning movement, leaving no excuse for failure.[129]

Meanwhile, Union signal stations reported to Grant that twenty-nine rail cars had been spotted chugging from Petersburg to Richmond between 6:00 p.m. and 6:45 p.m. Grant reported this to Meade at 8:10 p.m. with the observation, "This will make any surprise impossible, and may prevent our cavalry reaching the railroad." Grant decided to forward the information to Hancock and "let him do what he can in the morning in the way of turning the enemy and driving him from his present position. After that he will be best able to determine whether it will be well to push farther."[130]

At 9:00 p.m., Grant wired Halleck to explain the day's events. Grant seemed content to pick up on Hancock's theme that the lackluster performance was due to the exhaustion of the men. "The troops having marched at night were fatigued and did not follow up their success as they otherwise would," he rationalized. "Generals Sheridan and Kautz are now with Hancock, and the two will try in the morning to push the enemy back into Richmond or south of the James River." Little did they know what the Confederates had in store for them come sunrise.[131]

At the end of the day, when the smell of campfires began to waft through the air and soldiers blue and gray hunkered down for a warm and muggy night, the Union line consisted of Gibbon on the left near Bailey's Creek, two of Mott's Brigades in the center and Barlow on the right following the contours of the Long Bridge Road. Torbert's Division guarded the right flank at the Darby Farm, and De Trobriand's Brigade was refused and guarded the right flank of the corps.[132]

As Torbert's troopers settled in for the evening, they may have noticed that the place where they had set up camp was marked by different names on their maps. Some maps said they were at the "Enroughty" farm, while others had the name "Darby" listed on the same location. As it turned out, both names were correct, and in a bizarre twist, both names were pronounced the same way. To explain how this was so, one must look back to the 1750s, when the Enroughty family first purchased the land. When an Enroughty girl fell in love with a "plebeian scrub" with the last name Darby, her parents were incensed that she would marry someone deemed beneath her station. As a result, the girl was disowned and soon died. By the time Darby came to the end of his years, he had amassed quite a fortune and was willing to leave it to his snobby relations on one condition: they change their name to Darby. While the family wanted the money, they chafed at the proposed name change and came up with a solution that confused many mapmakers for generations to come. The family stated, "Let's keep on spelling it Enroughty and pronounce it Darby."[133]

"DRIVE HIM AWAY AND DESTROY HIS BRIDGES"

As word of the day's events trickled back to General Lee's headquarters, it was readily apparent that Kershaw needed to be heavily reinforced. Lee thus decided to send Major General Henry Heth's Third Corps division over to help Ewell and Kershaw's beleaguered forces. Lee looked to First Corps chieftain Lieutenant General Richard Heron Anderson to take overall control of the operation from the unreliable Ewell. Lee sent word to Anderson on the evening of the twenty-seventh, informing him that

> [a] dispatch just received from Genl Kershaw has determined me to send Genl Heth's division to reinforce him. I wish you to proceed to Deep Bottom & take command of the troops belonging to this army there. Examine the enemy's position, endeavor to ascertain his strength, and if practicable drive him away and destroy his bridges.[134]

When Anderson arrived at Chaffin's Bluff, he met with Ewell and was brought up to speed on what had transpired over the last twelve hours. Anderson later reported that "it was decided to attack the enemy's right at as early hour as was possible the following morning. All needful arrangements were made during the night.[135]

Heth remembered that the march from Petersburg was "aggravated by dusty roads" and was "as severe as any I have ever experienced," but he

Left: Major General Henry Heth. *Courtesy of the Library of Congress.*

Right: Lieutenant General Richard H. Anderson. *Courtesy of the Library of Congress.*

added that his men accomplished it "in order and without murmur." A soldier in his division murmured to his diary, "I was tempted several times to give up, but by an effort of will staggered along to the end. I cannot stand marching as formerly." Anderson planned for Heth to cover the New Market Line from Chaffin's down to New Market Heights while Kershaw moved four brigades farther left along Bailey's Creek. This would place the Confederates past Hancock's line and provide them an opportunity to attack and envelop his lines the next day. Heth's exhausted men arrived on the north side of the James after 2:00 a.m.[136]

And so it was that both sides settled down for the evening—both sides expecting to go on the offensive the next day…both sides expecting victory.

Chapter 6

COLLISION AT THE DARBY FARM

"IS THE TURNING MOVEMENT AN ABSOLUTE ONE?"

The sun began to peek over the horizon at 4:59 a.m. on the morning on Thursday, July 28. One hour later, with the temperature already well in the seventies, the 2,600 men of Birge's Brigade began to arrive at Deep Bottom. Perhaps a more aggressive commander would have greeted this as welcome news, but the apprehensive Hancock seemed determined to remain comfortably tucked in around his bridgehead. At 7:00 a.m., he sent word to Meade once again seeking confirmation that he was to resume the offensive. In language that seems to suggest that Hancock was trying to talk Meade into letting him off the hook, Hancock asked if the commanding general desired him to "make a vigorous attempt…with my command, at the risk of losing the line I hold in front of Bailey's Creek." After listing several reasons why such a move would be troublesome and risky, Hancock went so far as to query, "Is the turning movement an absolute one, or am I to make the movement at my discretion?" Armed with the knowledge that the Confederates had been reinforced and were dug in, all offensive spirit had fled the chieftain of the II Corps.[137]

Hancock's plight was not entirely illusory, however. Not only was he correct in worrying about the newly arrived Confederates, but he also had to contend with the fact that the Confederate line was more than two miles longer than he had at first suspected. In order to properly support

Sheridan's flanking maneuver, he would have to shift troops from the far left wing of the army farther east, exposing him to the risk of a Confederate force slipping past his left flank and cutting him off from the lower pontoon bridge. Birge's newcomers would have to compensate for this movement, but it is highly probable that Hancock was uncomfortable with troops from the disgraced XIX Corps protecting his vital escape route. With these factors in play, Hancock asked Meade for guidance. Just ten minutes after he received Hancock's request for clarification, the temperamental general shot back, "You have misunderstood my telegram." Meade went on to explain, "You will carry out [Grant's] views to the best of your ability, in accordance with your judgment and as circumstances may seem best. It is impossible for me at this distance, and in ignorance of the ground and position of your troops to give you detailed orders." Meade referred the question to Grant, who said that if Hancock could not achieve anything decisive that morning, he should pull back to Petersburg that night. Whether he liked it or not, Hancock was to go forward.[138]

In order to maximize his chances of success, Foster was ordered to make a demonstration in his front to attract as much attention from Ewell and Anderson as possible. Two hours before daylight, Foster and Hancock met to discuss the details of this arrangement, and Foster walked away from that meeting with a very clear idea in his mind that there would be an immediate attack at daybreak and that he should be ready to make his demonstration as soon as he heard firing on Hancock's front. When daylight came and went without the sounds of musketry, Foster complained to his superior, "I have had my troops under arms and ready since 3 a.m., but have heard no firing or no notice of an advance from General Hancock." Hancock eventually inquired if Foster had any troops at the lower pontoon bridge, to which the brigade commander replied that he did not. He volunteered to send a detachment from the 11th Maine to garrison the lower pontoon bridge and alerted Hancock that "my lookouts report the enemy busily engaged in throwing up works in the field where the gun-boat is shelling." Foster's men could not act until the main fight developed, however, and the responsibility for that rested in the hands of the cavalry.[139]

Sheridan gave the word for the blue cavaliers to hit the road at about 9:00 a.m. Gregg was to take the cavalry from Strawberry Plains and push east along Long Bridge Road to Riddell's Shop. From there, they would canter up the Charles City Road and extend the line to the right of Torbert's Division. Brigadier General Henry Davies had the lead, with Colonel J. Irvin Gregg's brigade following close behind. Torbert's two brigades still faced the

Confederates on Long Bridge Road west of the Darby House. To complete the mounted complement of mounted troops making this push, Brigadier General August V. Kautz's Army of the James division followed up behind Gregg's troopers. With Sheridan's troopers in motion, the stage was set for Lee's offensive to begin.[140]

Lieutenant General Anderson determined that Henry Heth's four fresh brigades would hold the New Market Line, while a battle group of four brigades was patched together from Kershaw's and Wilcox's divisions. The four brigades chosen were Lane's Brigade (under Colonel Robert V. Cowan, who had taken command of the brigade the day before), McGowan's Brigade (under Lieutenant Colonel J.F. Hunt), Kershaw's Brigade (under Colonel John Williford Henagan) and Brigadier General William T. Wofford's Georgia Brigade. Leading these four brigades into action was Brigadier General James Conner of Wilcox's division.

Anderson's objective in this assault was to turn Hancock's right and push him back to Curle's Neck, where he could be defeated in detail. Unfortunately for the Rebels, Anderson ordered no real reconnaissance to scout the Federal positions, so there was no way of knowing of the mounted threat moving his way in the form of Gregg and Kautz. In his haste, Anderson apparently did not even keep Lee apprised of the situation, forcing Lee to wire a hasty message to Ewell inquiring, "What is the enemy's force of cavalry? What do you propose to do? Are you directing operations?" If that was not bad enough, Anderson also somehow bungled the deployment of Wofford's Brigade—it was either intentionally left behind for some inexplicable reason or it did not get up in time to make the attack. Things were beginning to go awry before the first shot was fired in anger.[141]

If Anderson had ordered a reconnaissance of the ground over which his men were about to advance, he may have rethought his approach. After leaving the safety of the Confederate earthworks at Fussell's Mill, Conner's battle group had to traverse nearly two hundred yards of dense woods before hitting a county road that forked. The left fork of the road veered sharply to the east (its left), while the right fork swung sharply to the south. The path of its advance would then take it to a marsh along a branch that drained to White Oak Swamp. Once the men had negotiated all of this, they would enter a cornfield that was split almost completely in twain by a finger of woods jutting out from the opposite tree line in a northwesterly direction. Conner would be put to the test to see if he could keep his three brigades in good order as they advanced through such treacherous terrain.[142]

Brigadier General James Conner commanded the battle group that attacked the Darby Farm on July 28, 1864. He had two horses shot out from underneath him in the battle. *From Miller's* Photographic History of the Civil War.

Conner placed Cowan on the extreme right, with the 7th North Carolina on the left, followed by the 18th, 37th, 28th and 33rd North Carolina Regiments. Occupying the center was Hunt's Brigade. From right to left were the 1st and 14th South Carolina, Orr's Rifles and then the 13th and 12th South Carolina Regiments. Henagan's five regiments held the extreme left, though the order is uncertain. Federal artillery harassed the Confederates as they came out of their works. They stepped off at 10:00 a.m. with "official orders…to forward with the guide on the left." Halfway through the woods, part of Hunt's command and Henagan's full brigade encountered the forked county road. Despite an outcry from their officers, the men began to pour into the road, causing Hunt's Brigade to break up—the 1st and 14th South Carolina went with Cowan to the right, with the remainder of the brigade splitting off to the left with Henagan. With Conner's battle group sliced in half by the thumb of trees, two separate fights were about to develop.[143]

"We Had Our Asses Whip Off Us": The Fight for the Lower Field

The violent jolt that split Conner's attack force in half wreaked further havoc on the fragment consisting of Cowan and Hunt that had inadvertently maneuvered itself into the field west of the thumb of trees. As the ranks expanded and contracted, with officers haranguing the men to keep in line and dress their ranks, Hunt's boys shot out in front of Cowan, who had encountered the marsh and was "delayed a good while in the mud." Hunt's men emerged in the cornfield of the Darby Farm and discovered that they were facing off against the 2nd and 5th U.S. Cavalry of Merritt's Brigade all by themselves. Torbert's men had been trading potshots with Conner's men while they advanced through the woods, and when Hunt's men came out of the woods, they were shocked to find no one to their right and dismounted cavalry directly in their front—as one Rebel recalled, "the confusion increased, as a matter of course."[144]

Unperturbed, the 1st and 14th South Carolina pushed toward the Federals, loading and firing as they went. A startled Union trooper in the 1st Maine Cavalry jotted down in his diary that the Confederates "came down across an open field without a particle of skirmish line. It was a splendid sight. Their colors were flying, drums beating and the officers could be heard dressing the ranks. They knew only cavalry was in front of them and doubtless counted on an easy and bloodless victory."[145]

As the Rebels came on, Union skirmisher George B. Sanford of the 1st U.S. Cavalry described what happened to the skirmish line: "When the rebel line advanced we fell back to the crest of a hill, behind which we lay down to get a little rest. The hill overlooked a valley perhaps three-fourths of a mile in width and bordered by a thick woods." As a Southerner in Hunt's Brigade recalled, "The enemy fled before us, taking refuge partly on the edge of the opposite farm (some three hundred yards off), partly in a strip of wood that ran up, from the north, to the crest of the open ridge we occupied." Sanford watched as the Confederates in the woods "halted—apparently to dress their lines, and we got a chance to reform also and to get our lines rectified. Soon they advanced again and as they came out into the open ground, we saw at once that it was an infantry force that we were fighting." A sergeant in the 6th New York described the situation back at the main line:

> *Suddenly the sharp rattle of musketry was heard in our front and before we could realize that we were attacked, our pickets were coming in closely followed by a heavy force of Confederate infantry; our bugle sounded "Stand to horse" but our horses were mostly unsaddled and had we been mounted we could not have fought to any advantage, for the ground was cut up and intersected by ditches, fences and scattering clumps of trees.*[146]

In the meantime, Cowan encountered not only the swamp he had to negotiate but also Federal skirmishers. Captain James G. Harris of the 7th North Carolina stated that he moved with his "command about one-fourth of a mile, and came unexpectedly on the enemy's out post occupied by cavalry." Before he could order his men to fire, the skirmishers fired off a quick volley and immediately fled. Harris recalled that they were "soon out of view, covered by the dense undergrowth of the surrounding woods." Harris quickly caught up to the fleeing Yankees, and a running battle ensued, with the men of the 7th availing "themselves of such protection as was offered by the friendly trees, and returned the enemy's fire with spirit."[147]

William H.A. Speer, the commander of the 28th North Carolina, similarly reported, "[I]n moving forward my Reg. came in contact with the enemy in a very thick swamp but drove them out into a cornfield. In getting through the swamp the Reg't was broken up in formation to some extent, but reformed

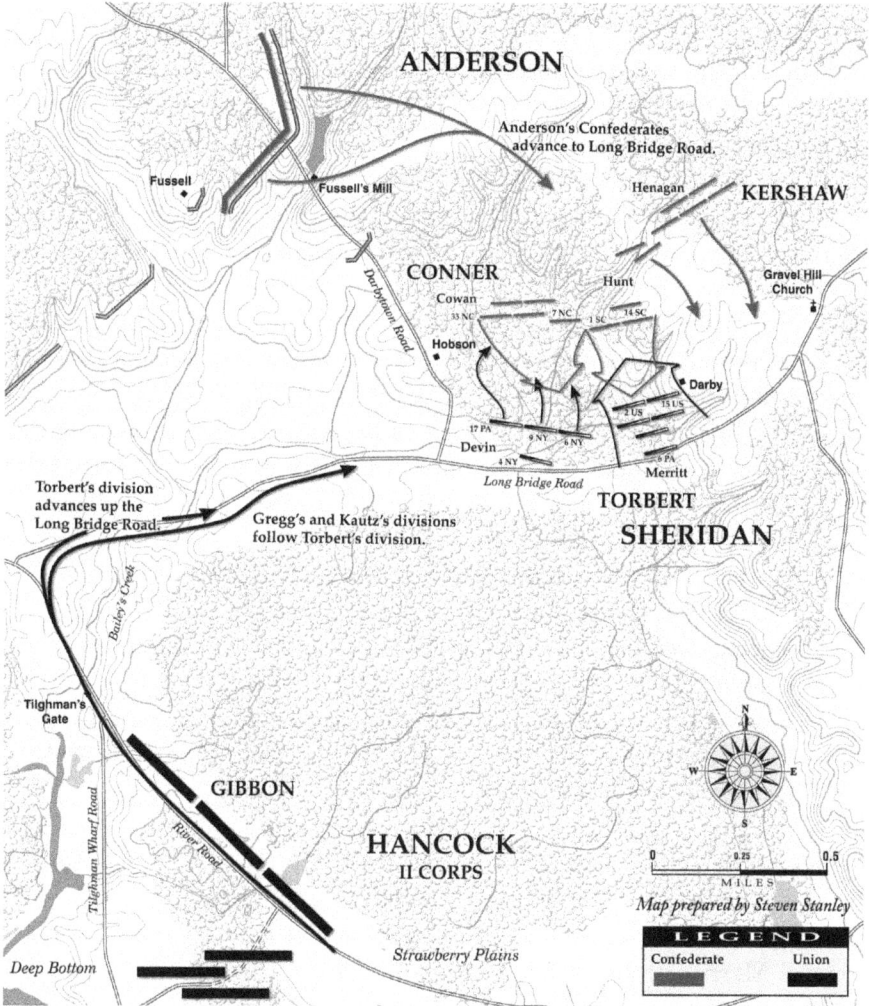

The Confederates attack the Darby Farm, July 28, 1864. *Map by Steven Stanley.*

to some degree after getting into the corn field." With this further cause for delay now gone, Cowan's men pushed out of the woods into the open clearing, where Hunt's men were already engaged.[148]

Trying to catch up to Hunt's men, Cowan ordered his men to march by the right flank, throwing his line into even more confusion as some regiments surged ahead, some collided with one another and some could not comply with the order because they were still entangled with Merritt's skirmishers.

The 18th and 37th North Carolina were able to pull off the maneuver, but the 28th and 33rd could not because they were being fired into. Seeing that Hunt was out in front all by himself, Cowan passed down the order for his men to advance at the double-quick.

Major Jackson L. Bost of the 37th North Carolina reported that the order to double-quick "caused the regts to lap over each other"—the 18th overlapped the 37th, and the 37th, in turn, overlapped the 28th. Bost reported to Cowan, who "happened to be present" and was ordered to take the 37th out of its current position and shift it to the extreme right of the brigade. In the confusion of the advance—in which men were bumping into one another and the line was moving back and forth like an accordion while under the fire of the enemy's pickets—Bost was not able to execute this order. Some men could not understand why they would be moved to the right when they had initially been told to guide to the left. Bost explained:

> [I] *only succeeded in getting a portion to move to the right the rest having gone on with the Brigade and some became mixed up with* [Hunt's] *brigade. With that I could make understand to move to right of the brigade I march by the flank. to the right having just myself to brake them off from the line and just in the rear, and tell them all along the line what to do and before I had gone far I was fired into from the right & rear which confused the most of the man and made them think they were flanked.*

Thus, only a fraction of the 37th followed Bost to the right of the line, causing more mayhem and confusion in an already deteriorating advance.[149]

Meanwhile, the men of the 7th North Carolina were able to push back some of Merritt's troopers, but the Federals had an answer for them. Colonel Thomas C. Devin was ordered by Torbert to file down to Merritt's left, and this put him squarely in position to deal with Cowan's oncoming troops. The 9th New York Cavalry was sent into the woods directly to Cowan's right with orders to fire into the flank of the Rebels when they drew near. Newell Cheney, the historian of the 9th, recalled, "The men quickly formed and moved by companies and squadrons into line along the sides of the open field." Corporal Nelson Taylor detected an air of arrogance in the way in which Cowan's men came at the horse soldiers, writing after that battle that "they thought Cavalry would not stand [a] bayonet charge." When the 9th sidled into position, General Torbert, watching their well-executed deployment, asked, "What regiment is that?" Colonel Devin, swelling with pride, answered, "The 9th New York…You will hear them yell directly." With the 9th on the move, Devin ordered Major James A. Hall and his 6th New York Cavalry to fire into the face of Cowan's men when he heard the 9th New York's carbines begin to blaze away.[150]

By now, Cowan and Hunt were in the open and moving in the same direction, although, as J.F.J. Caldwell of the 1st South Carolina later said, Cowan "moved up, but did not connect with us, or even get quite on a line with us." As the men advanced toward the crest of the hill, where the Federal skirmishers had initially fled, another derangement of the line occurred at the marshy swale at the foot of the hill. The 1st and 14th South Carolina lost contact with each other as they began the ascent—a situation made worse by the fact that a two-hundred-yard gap separated Cowan from the two disconnected regiments.[151]

When Cowan's men were within two hundred yards of the Darby Farm, the 9th New York sprung its trap. Newell Cheney recalled how "when within short carbine range the 9th opened with a rapid carbine fire. The enemy seemed bewildered." The 17th Pennsylvania Cavalry was fed into the fight to the left of the 9th New York, putting it in a position to fire into the flank and rear of the 33rd North Carolina. The commanding officer of the 33rd reported:

> We were subject to an enfilade fire but held our position until attacked on the right flank & rear. I would here beg leave to state that the officers & men under my command acted most gallantly at this particular juncture fighting the enemy at about only ten paces distance some instances nearer.[152]

Distracted by the threat to its flank, the 33rd was completely undone when the 6th New York chose the most opportune time to open up in the faces of the Tarheels. A noncommissioned officer in the 6th observed that "[a]s on previous occasions, our breech-loading carbines proved their superiority—at short range—over the muzzle loading rifles of the enemy, for every shot that they fired we could give two in return." Panic seized the beleaguered men of the 33rd North Carolina.

With the Confederates frozen in indecision, the New Yorkers abandoned the shelter of the woods and ran pell-mell straight into the Confederates. The historian of the 9th New York described what happened next:

> The enemy…halted, then faced about and moved rapidly back followed by the men of the 9th using their carbines and revolvers with deadly effect. The 6th New York was on the right and the 17th Pennsylvania on the left, but did

Left: Brigadier General Wesley Merritt. *Courtesy of the Library of Congress.*

Right: Colonel Thomas C. Devin. *Courtesy of the Library of Congress.*

> *not advance so rapidly. Just then Col. [George S.] Nichols rode up onto the field and shouted, "Halt," "Halt," "Come back you crazy fools," but when he saw the men were bent on finishing up the job they had begun, he shouted, "Charge then — —" "Charge to Hell if you want to."*

A correspondent from the *New York Times* was as astounded as the troopers:

> [S]*uddenly emerging from a piece of woods, and opening a brisk fire within pistol range, created such a panic that the enemy did not wait for the safest route by which to retreat, but exposed their whole flank in the movement. Officers seized their pistols and fired, regardless of the consequences, and the men, for half an hour, kept up a rapid fire from carbines and pistols.*[153]

With dismounted Yankees charging in and blazing away in front and flank, the 33rd North Carolina began to break and scurry back to the protection of the field over which it had just charged. A private in the 33rd wrote in a letter home that the Yankees "flank us an cross fired on us and runn us back threw the terable Swamp." Complaining that the 28th and 37th North Carolina "afforded me no assistance whatever," Captain William Callais officially ordered the regiment to rally "at [the] lower edge of the corn field." With its neighboring regiment coming apart at the seams, the 28th North Carolina was placed in the predicament from which the 33rd had just begun to exit. Conner saw his right flank disintegrating and ordered the 7th North Carolina to form a line "perpendicular to the old one," and this was done quickly.[154]

To make matters worse for the Carolinians, Merritt reinforced his success by committing his reserve—the 6th Pennsylvania Cavalry—into the fight. The Pennsylvanians charged furiously toward the oncoming Confederates at the double-quick until reaching the buildings of the Darby Farm. At that point, "the command was then given to charge, and the forward movement was promptly taken up by the other regiments in our line, and by the 2d brigade on our left, and together, we drove this North Carolina brigade off the field." Lieutenant Colonel Speer of the 28th reasoned that "being flanked thus by the enemy and being still exposed to the sever flank fire...I ordered my men to fall back to a ridge to the rear." Speer added, "I never saw the men fight with more spirit and gallantry in my life." Speer failed to mention that the battle flag for the 28th was captured during the retreat by Private Samuel L. Malleck, Company I, 9th New York Cavalry.[155]

Cowan's front was now riddled with holes, with the 33rd and 28th North Carolina fleeing the field, the 7th now facing to the west with its left flank completely exposed to Yankee carbine and pistol fire, the 18th advancing steadily on and the 37th North Carolina still in the midst of executing Cowan's order to move to the right. One Tarheel observing Colonel Cowan said that the brigade commander "don sum of his big Swaring because the Regt was so scattered."[156]

Seeing the desperate predicament of the Confederates, Merritt ordered his entire brigade to charge. A correspondent for the *Baltimore Clipper* looked on as the Reserve Brigade of Torbert's Division "fell furiously upon the... exposed flank of the enemy." This charge along the entire front severely damaged the 1st and 14th South Carolina as well. Caldwell recalled that "so warm was the fire from these, and so strong the conviction of failure, that we gradually gave clear back, across the open field." Pursued by Merritt's fevered horse soldiers, they fell back in disarray to a rail fence at the northern edge of the cornfield. This fence stuck out in the mind of at least one Yankee unfamiliar with the types of enclosures preferred by farmers such as the Darbys. He reminisced, "The Virginia rail fence is an institution peculiar to the 'sacred soil' it is made entirely of rails laid one upon another in a zig-zag line, and affords considerable protection from rifle bullets, as every soldier who fought in the Army of the Potomac knows." The Confederates were quick to put this advantage to use.[157]

Throwing themselves over the fence and lying flat on the ground, the Southerners slid their muskets through the crevices of the fence and opened "a close and deadly fire" upon Merritt's men. The remnant of the 28th North Carolina also took refuge behind the fence, but according to Lieutenant Colonel Speer, the unit "was unable to hold this position long." General Conner recognized that this fence was the best hope he had for holding the Federals back, and rallying his demoralized men, he spurred his horse toward it to encourage them. Conner's mount took a bullet midstride and, according to Conner, "went about 80 yards and dropped." Unmoved, Conner took his adjutant's horse and rode it along the lines until it, too, was shot by two Yankee bullets. J.F.J. Caldwell saw the general "defying the enemy's line with his pistol," but it was all for naught. A "mortified" Conner concluded, "It was a pretty hot place and I had run considerable risk for when the brigade of Lanes broke I rode before them trying to rally them. How I escaped I can't tell. Nothing but the providence of God saved me for the bullets were flying thick and fast and I was pretty conspicuous as I rode forward waving my hat."

Members of the 1st U.S. Cavalry in camp in early 1864. Private Timothy O'Connor of Company E would win the Medal of Honor for his actions at the Darby Farm on July 28, 1864. *From Miller's* Photographic History of the Civil War.

Officers of the 28th North Carolina. Colonel William H.A. Speer is in the upper left corner. From *Clark's* North Carolina Regiments, *vol. 2.*

Conner's bravery set a good example, and his men checked the bluecoats for a moment, but time was quickly running out. Sensing that victory was at hand, Federal buglers sounded the attack once more.[158]

The 7th and 18th North Carolina had just retreated to the safety of the fence when the Regular Brigade hit them full tilt. Lieutenant Colonel John McGill, commanding the 18th North Carolina, stated that "my Regiment had to fall back under a most galling fire, and I fear that several of my men who are now missing were either wounded or killed as several were to start to fall back and have not been seen since." Among those he feared missing was Corporal David M. Barefoot of Company H, who "received the colors and bore them at the front until I ordered the Regiment to retreat." As it turned out, Barefoot had encountered a young trooper in the 1st U.S. Cavalry named Timothy O'Connor, who was about to win his nation's highest honor: the Congressional Medal of Honor.[159]

Timothy O'Connor was originally from County Kerry, Ireland, but settled in Chicago once he came to the United States. When the dark specter of war cast its shadow over his newly adopted country, O'Connor answered the call and enlisted in Company F, 23rd Illinois, in 1862. When the 23rd was kept out of the famous battles of 1862, O'Connor jumped ship and enlisted in Company E, 1st U.S. Cavalry. By the time of First Deep Bottom, O'Connor was a high private who found himself in the vanguard of Merritt's counterattack. Before long, he was looking poor Corporal Barefoot in the eye and wrestling the regimental colors out of his hands. For this daring action, O'Connor was awarded the Medal of Honor. His citation notes that he was awarded the medal "for extraordinary heroism on 28 July 1864, while serving with Company E, 1st U.S. Cavalry, in action at Malvern, Virginia, for capture of flag of the 18th North Carolina Infantry (Confederate States of America)."[160]

The last stand of Cowan and Hunt's men was over, and the Carolinians high-tailed it back to where they had started from two hours earlier, forming a new line of battle just in case the Federal troopers wanted to continue their pursuit. Captain Callais of the 33rd North Carolina concluded his official report of this battle by stating that "[t]he regiment was…immediately afterward given orders by Col. Cowan to fall back about sixty or seventy yards & form in line of battle…which order was promptly executed." A soldier in the ranks of the 33rd named Augustin E. Shore had a different take on the action: "We had our asses whip off us if the truth was knone."[161]

"YOU MAY ALL BE FOOLS ENOUGH TO STAY HERE BUT I'LL NOT": THE FIGHT FOR THE UPPER FIELD

There was plenty of whipping to be had in the upper field as well, and both sides got a taste of it before the fighting was through. Just as Conner's attack force was emerging from its works at Fussell's Mill, Brigadier General Henry E. Davies Jr. was advancing in column of fours up the Long Bridge Road with his two advance regiments, the 10th New York Cavalry and the 6th Ohio Cavalry. This was the vanguard of Gregg's Division, which had been tasked with spearheading the long-awaited turning movement of Sheridan's cavalry. Colonel J. Irvin Gregg—the division commander's first cousin—was in the center, with Kautz's Army of the James Division bringing up the rear. Gregg's force arrived just as the *cracks* from Merritt's skirmishers began to fill the air with the sound of carbine fire.

When Davies's first two regiments rounded a turn in the road, they were temporarily lost from sight. The 1st Pennsylvania neared the turn in the road when Conner's left wing—the remainder of Hunt's and all of Henagan's Brigades, numbering around 1,700 men—emerged from the woods. Since this offshoot of Conner's battle group was coming in at an angle near where the Long Bridge Road curved to the northeast, Hunt and Henagan's men had a smaller distance to cover before they encountered the blue-clad cavalrymen.

Gregg later recalled that "the attack was made by the enemy in line of battle, without skirmishers, and across the only open field in the vicinity...The dense woods surrounding prevented any formation of mounted men." The division commander quickly ordered his men to dismount and took charge of Davies's men since the general was "with the advance

Brigadier General David McM. Gregg skillfully led his men against Confederate infantry at the Darby Farm. *Courtesy of the Library of Congress.*

when the attack was made." One man in every four was tasked with leading the horses to the safety of the rear, thus reducing Gregg's effective force to about 2,600 hardy troopers. Gregg also shot out orders for the 1st New Jersey and 1st Massachusetts to move to the left and occupy the thumb of trees "to prevent the enemy from breaking in between us and the First Division." The 1st Pennsylvania Cavalry was then placed on the right in the road. To the right of the 1st Pennsylvania were two three-inch ordnance rifles under Lieutenant William N. Dennison's Light Battery A, 2nd U.S. Artillery.[162]

Dennison was an outstanding veteran artillerist who had gotten Gregg's men out of tough scrapes in the past. The senior horse artillerist on the field, Captain Alanson Randol, may have had a queasy feeling in his stomach, since he was only several hundred yards from where he had lost a battery two years earlier at the Battle of Glendale. As the Confederates advanced, Dennison's pieces "knocked gaps through their exposed columns, which were almost instantly filled by closing up, while the First and Second Pennsylvania and First Massachusetts responded with their carbines in front." Gregg was happy to see that the combined fire from Davies and Dennison "checked temporarily the advance of the enemy." Davies said that his men pushed the enemy back to the woods "in confusion," where they regrouped for another try.[163]

Davies moved quickly to organize his defense, placing the 10th New York next to Dennison's guns and the 6th Ohio on the far right. No sooner had Lieutenant Neil A. Bushnell of the 6th Ohio been placed in line than "presently our attention was attracted to the head of this rebel column as it emerged from the woods about thirty rods from us, marching out into the open field and forming line facing us." Hunt's men had come back, and they wanted Dennison's guns.[164]

Lieutenant James "Newt" Martin of the 3rd South Carolina watched as his comrades "charged a cross a cornfield about (400) yard for the purpose of

Captain Alanson M. Randol lost a cannon at the Darby Farm only eight hundred yards from the spot where he had lost a battery in 1862. *Courtesy of the Library of Congress.*

Lieutenant William Dennison (far right) used his cannons to hold back the Confederate onslaught as long as possible. *Courtesy of the Library of Congress.*

capturing a Batery which was dun in good style by the 13 [South Carolina]." As the regiment advanced, a member of the 7th South Carolina complained that the Yankees were "playing on us all the while with a battery of artillery." The Confederates hit hard, and Gregg's men were hard-pressed to fend them off. Davies saw that this charge was "made in greater force and with greater determination" and rode back and forth along his line, trying to plug gaps and encourage his men to stand their ground. Being one of the few Federals on horseback, Davies made an inviting target, and he quickly had two horses shot out from underneath him and received a slight wound to his foot. The Rebels surged forward and began driving the Federal cavalrymen back. The men of the 12th and 13th South Carolina of Hunt's Brigade zeroed in on Dennison's battery, causing the onlooking Gregg to order it withdrawn. Although the order was delivered, for some unknown reason Dennison's artillerists kept firing, prompting an apprehensive Gregg to send another courier to tell Dennison to limber up and retreat as fast as possible.[165]

By now, the Confederates were in the trees on either side of the Long Bridge Road, causing the 1st New Jersey and 1st Massachusetts to retire. Lieutenant Bushnell of the 6th Ohio recalled that "as soon as the rebel column faced us, we gave them a parting shot and 'lit out.'" Dennison's beleaguered guns were now virtually unsupported. The lieutenant explained in his official report:

> [O]ur line was obliged to retire. I retired all of my battery, with the exception of one 3-inch gun, which I kept in position in order to check the enemy until General Davies' brigade could leave the field. I succeeded in doing this, when the enemy, with two divisions of infantry, charged my gun. When he (enemy) was within fifty yards of my gun I limbered it up and sent my cannoneers to the rear, in order to get them out of the galling fire which was at that time concentrated upon my piece.

The two "divisions" that Dennison saw were actually just the 12th and 13th South Carolina, which closed in rapidly, eager to have their names added to the roll of honor for capturing a Federal battery. It is important to note that, other than seizing a foe's colors, the capture of an enemy battery was the quickest way to be immortalized in Civil War armies. Twenty-year-old Sergeant Adam W. Ballenger of Company C, 13th South Carolina, was familiar with this fact and decided that now was the time to risk his life for glory.[166]

One can only imagine the shock Ballenger's comrades must have felt when they saw the impetuous youngster run out ahead of the column to take on Dennison's entire battery. Still, the sergeant's gamble paid off, and a well-aimed volley killed the two wheel horses that were taking Dennison's final piece off the field. Dennison begged for help, and a detachment of fifteen men under the command of Major Avery of the 10th New York rushed to the gun and tried to move it by hand, as there weren't enough horses left to take the gun off the field.[167]

Sergeant Adam Washington Ballenger shown later in life. Ballenger fought with the 13th South Carolina at the Darby Farm and won a Confederate Medal of Honor for his actions there. *From Landrum's* History of Spartanburg County.

At this point, Ballenger ran up to the cannon and jumped on it, causing the driver of one of the few remaining horses to "jump off on the tongue between the horses and make his escape." Incredibly, Ballenger then "jumped off the piece, cut loose the traces and unfastened the off-horse, which he mounted." Ballenger enlisted help in hauling off the piece; several men grabbed the prolonge and began leading the prize back to the rear. By now, the rest of the two South Carolina regiments were with him, and they dealt with the detail of the 10th New York, which put up a valiant effort to recapture the guns. Major Avery's men put forth "the most superhuman efforts" to reclaim the gun and "charged repeatedly the advancing columns of the enemy," but it was too little too late. Avery ordered his shattered detachment to fall back and catch up with Dennison and the rest of the fleeing Federal column. Colonel Hunt saw all of this transpire and credited it to Ballenger, stating, "I consider our success due in a great measure to the conduct of Sergt. Ballenger."[168]

The loss of Dennison's gun must have galled Captain Randol, having now lost more cannons on this unlucky ground, but he was quick to absolve the intrepid young lieutenant of all blame. Writing a week after the battle, Randol explained in his report:

Lieutenant Dennison did everything in his power to save his gun, and gallantly stood by it to the last, having one horse killed under him and another wounded. I attribute the loss of the gun to the fact that the enemy could advance under excellent cover to within short rifle range of the position we occupied, to the killing of the two wheel horses, and to the want of a regularly designated support.

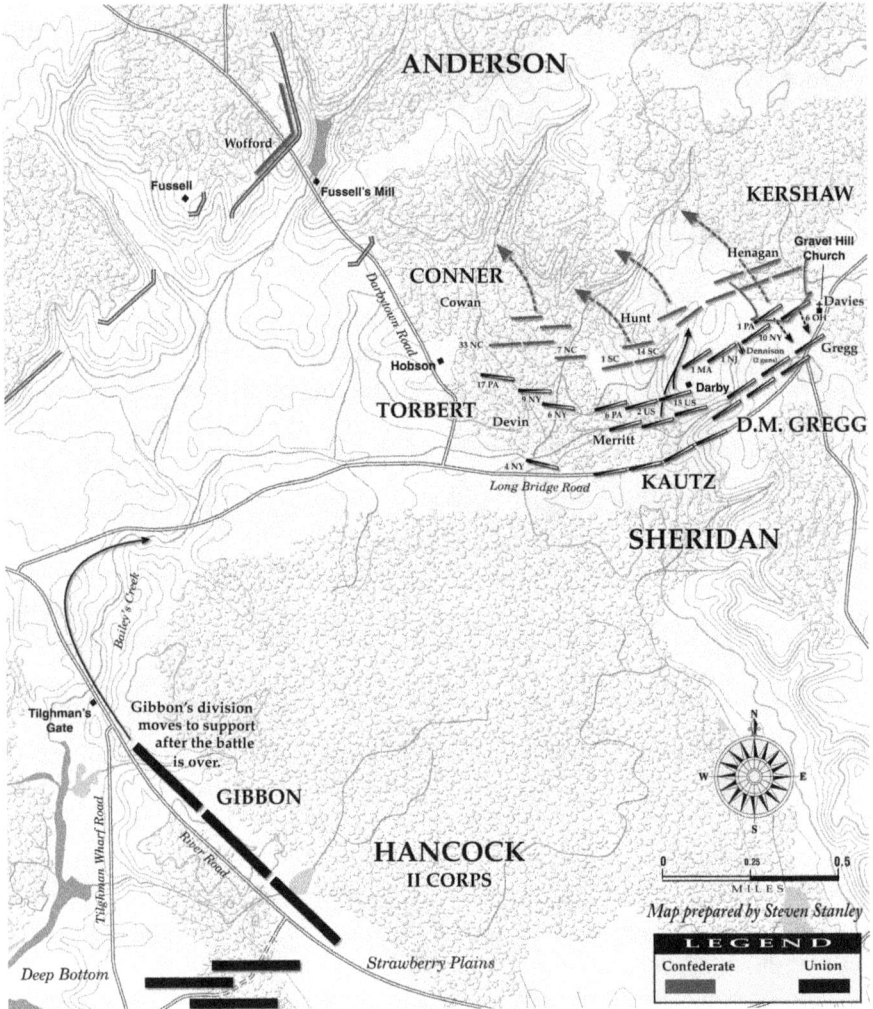

The Federal counterattack, July 28, 1864. *Map by Steven Stanley.*

Dennison's sacrifice enabled Davies to extract his brigade without serious loss.[169]

While Hunt and Henagan's men were ecstatic over their hard-won victory over the Yankee artillery and cavalry, their revelry was cut short by the realization that their comrades in the lower field had not been as successful. Looking over to that section of the field, G.W. Bussey of the 7th South Carolina was shocked when he "saw a strong force of the enemy almost between us and the other portion of our line." One startled soldier in the 3rd South Carolina was heard to exclaim, "My God, men look yonder. You may all be fools enough to stay here but I'll not." The realization then set in that "the other brigades had failed to drive them in front as we did." The exhaustion of the preceding marching and fighting also caught up to the fatigued Carolinians. Lieutenant Martin of the 3rd South Carolina wrote home that "[t]he Sun was verry hot. One of our men fainted just as we stopped but by the application of cold wayter was soon restored."[170]

With the remainder of Gregg's Division nearby and Kautz's troopers beginning to arrive, the Confederates could not stay in the field east of the Darby House. "We had to fall back, which was done in considerable confusion," stated a scorned soldier in the 3rd South Carolina Battalion. "When we got back to woods we had advance from, there seemed to be a dozen different stands of colors. Scarce two men of same company together. All was confusion. Some said the cavalry was in our rear." General Anderson joined his men once they had fallen back and established their new line, and his presence seemed to have a calming effect on the men. Anderson expected a counterattack at any minute and tried to get his stunned troops ready to meet it.[171]

Conner had taken severe casualties with not much to show for it. The general reported 228 casualties in Hunt's Brigade alone. In Cowan's Brigade, the 7th North Carolina lost 25 casualties, the 18th North Carolina reported 21 casualties, the 28th lost 38 men and the 37th North Carolina reported 32 men killed, wounded and missing. No figures were given for the 33rd North Carolina. Reliable casualty figures for Henagan's men have not been found, although the chaplain of the 15th South Carolina did note that some of the "best and most useful Christians in the brigade were lost." A Federal surgeon who established a field hospital near Malvern Hill after the battle noted that Confederates had left many of their wounded on the field. In all, it is estimated that the Confederates suffered 377 casualties in this attack, while the Federals suffered approximately 200. After an action of only thirty minutes, Conner's battle group withdrew, leaving 30 dead and a dozen wounded on the field.[172]

Chapter 7

TIME SLIPS AWAY

"GENERAL HANCOCK, EITHER I AM VERY STUPID THIS MORNING OR YOU ARE UNINTELLIGIBLE"

In the aftermath of Conner's precipitous flight back to the safety of the wood line, Gregg ordered a hot pursuit of Sergeant Ballenger and the South Carolinians who had made off with Lieutenant Dennison's cannon. General Gregg recalled that "as soon as the narrow wood road upon which the gun was carried off by the enemy was discovered, a mounted regiment was sent to effect its recapture." Sadly, said the victorious commander, "this was not accomplished." What was accomplished, on the other hand, was a tentative mounted pursuit of Conner's entire force. With Kautz now up and in position to support him, Colonel J. Irvin Gregg ordered a counterattack along the entire line. Before this course of action could be pursued, however, his younger cousin rescinded the order.[173]

"Mounted regiments were pushed forward rapidly in pursuit," stated the division commander, "but the enemy, under cover of the dense pines which mounted troops could not penetrate, effected their escape, leaving about 30 of their dead and a number of wounded on the field." In spite of this, Sheridan was still in a favorable position to mount a successful counterattack. Since the flinty Irishman filed no official report on the battle, it will forever remain unclear why he did not do so.[174]

Back at Hancock's headquarters near Sweeney's Potteries, the commanding general of the Union expedition anxiously awaited news regarding the sounds of musketry he had been hearing since early in the morning. It had taken nearly an hour for a courier dispatched from Sheridan to reach Hancock and warn him of Conner's 10:00 a.m. attack. Hancock ordered Gibbon to prepare his Second Division to move at a moment's notice and to send out a few of his staff officers to scout the shortest route to reach the embattled cavalry. Gibbon complied with this order, sending out some of his staff and seeing what developed next. What Gibbon did not know is that Hancock had expected Gibbon to move out as soon as he was shown the quickest path to Sheridan's troopers.

After thirty minutes, Hancock rode up to see Gibbon and his men placidly holding their position, completely oblivious to the fact that their commander expected them to be well on their way to relieve the cavalry. An apoplectic Hancock rode up to Gibbon and tersely asked, "General Gibbon, is your division in motion?"

A serene Gibbon responded, "No, sir, I have received no orders to move it."

"I gave you an order half an hour ago to move it up," Hancock exploded.

Gibbon stood his ground and explained, "General, I received no such order, but simply one to hold it in readiness to move which was given and my troops are awaiting orders."

When Hancock continued to push the issue and imply that Gibbon was being insubordinate, a flabbergasted Gibbon finally told his commander, "General Hancock, either I am very stupid this morning or you are unintelligible, for I certainly did not understand you to give any such order."

The ugly exchange drew to a close when Hancock asked Major William Mitchell of his own staff to prove that he was right. An ill-at-ease Mitchell must have sweated through every layer of his uniform when he sheepishly responded that Hancock had only told Gibbon to hold his division "in readiness." Clearly bested, Hancock gave the order he thought he had given previously, and Gibbon was quickly en route to the beleaguered cavalry.[175]

"I SHALL FIGHT IN THE INTRENCHMENTS WHICH I TOOK YESTERDAY"

This testy back and forth between two generals who had been amicable up until this time shows the stress that Hancock was under. Plagued by fears of being cut off from the bridgehead, his actions after Sheridan's success were strictly defensive in nature. He expected a Confederate attack at any moment that would emanate from the Darbytown Road, designed to cut him off from the lower pontoon bridge. At 12:40 p.m., Hancock wired Grant and Meade:

> *The enemy seems to be extending his line a little farther to his left (our right). If a formidable attack is made on me by the enemy this p.m. I shall fight in the intrenchments which I took yesterday, and on Strawberry Plains, because my present line is too long to guard. I think it possible that I may be attacked next on the Central [Darbytown] road, but have a brigade watching it; Barlow's division near at hand.*[176]

Indeed, Hancock had ordered Barlow to the Charles City Road in case another phantom Confederate force chose to strike from that direction. Around the same time that Hancock updated Grant on the situation, Gibbon's Division completed its two-mile march accompanied by Captain Edwin Dow's 6th Maine Artillery—on loan from Mott's Division arriving just after the fighting had concluded. He took position on Barlow's right along Long Bridge Road. Gibbon's infantrymen filed into position, occupying the ground previously held by Torbert's men, his left flank resting on Long Bridge Road, with the 6th Maine Artillery placed on his right. Gibbon's men began taking pieces of the fence that had played such an important role in the preceding battle and creating a makeshift breastwork out of them. In the meantime, Sheridan ordered Gregg to move his division back and "form it on the right of General Torbert," who had been ordered rearward to the previous site of Gregg's headquarters at Strawberry Plains.[177]

At 12:35 p.m., farther to the west, General Foster was given the go-ahead to stage the demonstration that he had been prepared to execute nine hours earlier. In addition to this demonstration, Foster was also told to station a garrison at the works around the lower bridge. Hancock bolstered the defenses at the lower bridge by sending Major John W. Hazard to place his guns there. The heavily utilized 11th Maine was tasked by Foster to guard the bridge. Hazard transferred Captain Nelson Ames's Battery G, 1st New York Light Artillery, from Jones' Neck to the position. They would eventually be joined by Gregg's and Torbert's troopers.[178]

To help Foster tie down the Confederate troops and demoralize them, USS *Agawam* and USS *Mendota* bombarded the Confederate positions. Navy captain Melancton Smith reported:

The enemy made a demonstration on General Foster's front and the Agawam *opened fire, but with what effect it has not been ascertained. Commander Nichols, of the* Mendota, *reports that he fired at intervals of seventeen minutes and that General Hancock informed him that his shelling was very effective and of great assistance to his operations.*[179]

After the gunboats began firing, Foster sent out a skirmish line, consisting of the 100th New York and the 24th Massachusetts, supported by the 1st Connecticut Light Battery. These skirmishers advanced, causing the Confederate pickets to scamper back to their main line, but no major fighting developed. Foster continued to push up to the New Market Line, with the gunboats lobbing their massive shells a few times each hour, until Major Benjamin C. Ludlow of Hancock's staff told him not to bother, since Hancock wasn't going to attack anyway.[180]

"From All Accounts Lee Is Considerably Alarmed"

On the Confederate side of things, Robert E. Lee was anxious to learn if his reinforcements north of the river were having the desired effect. When Finley Anderson of the *New York Herald* told his readers that "[f]rom all accounts Lee is considerably alarmed," he was more accurate than even he probably knew. Lee's forces were desperately extended, prompting the great Lee biographer Douglas Southall Freeman to later ponder, "Perhaps it was at this time, when he was strained to the utmost to defend so long a line, that Lee began to doubt whether it was wise to attempt indefinitely to hold Richmond with his weakened army." Lee's anxiety was alleviated a bit when he received a dispatch from Ewell, in response to his earlier query regarding who was in charge of the Confederate effort to push Hancock back:

I consider myself directing operations as much as circumstances permit. I infer that the enemy's force of cavalry is formidable. General Anderson has been fighting it and General Gary has sent repeatedly for more troops. I have just returned from near our left. Pemberton has been ordered to Richmond and the right of my line is weak. The enemy have erected batteries in front of New Market and threaten along Four-Mile Run. I have not seen Anderson since late last night...I am about to return.[181]

Anderson may have been surprised to know that "Old Bald Head" was in charge, since the maneuver that led to the debacle at the Darby Farm was his idea. Having been rebuffed in this attempt, Anderson decided not to venture from the safety of his new line again until he received reinforcements, which he presumed would be sent shortly. Reporting to General Lee after the campaign had concluded, Anderson explained:

> *Learning that reinforcements were coming further operations were deferred until their arrival and to guard against any attempts which the enemy might make in the meantime on the New Market Road the four brigades were withdrawn…to their former position near Fussel's Mill.*[182]

Had the Union commanders been in any sort of aggressive mood, they would have seen that Kershaw's withdrawal left the Charles City Road wide open as an avenue of attack. To block the road, Anderson hurriedly sent for General Gary's understrength cavalry brigade. Gary's men speedily withdrew from Riddell's Shop and rode hard and fast to Deep Run, where they began to build breastworks. At 3:00 p.m., Anderson called on Ewell to send him Pemberton's artillery units to come to his aid by filling in along the Williamsburg Road to block a potential Yankee assault from that direction. Heth's newly arrived division remained idle all day, staying in its earthworks and dodging shells from the Union gunboats.[183]

"I Am Yet in Hopes of Turning This Diversion to Account"

General Anderson was not the only person with Confederate reinforcements on the brain—Hancock, too, was concerned about an enemy buildup that might descend on him at any moment. At 1:50 p.m., an "intelligent" Confederate prisoner, apparently born in the state of Ohio, informed Hancock that Bushrod Johnson's Tennessee Division, along with George Pickett's and Charles W. Field's Divisions, were north of the James. Hancock sent word to Barlow at 2:40 p.m. that he was to pull back as soon as Gibbon's men withdrew to "a position somewhat in rear of his present position, toward the open plain" near Tilghman's Gate. The three divisions fell back a few hours later, leaving a small line of pickets posted along the Long Bridge Road.[184]

Now the Federal infantry was more or less where it had begun the day from: the line they had taken from Humphreys's men the day before. From left to right, Birge's men held from the point where Bailey's Creek enters the James to Sweeney's Potteries. Mott's men extended to Birge's right, followed by Barlow and then Gibbon, with De Trobriand's brigade of Mott's Division protecting the right flank of the corps.[185]

At 3:15 p.m., Lieutenant Colonel Comstock notified Hancock that Grant, Meade and several staff officers had boarded a steamer and were headed to the lower pontoon bridge. The party arrived at 5:00 p.m., and the consultation was apparently brief. Lieutenant Colonel Lyman recorded in his journal how Meade's chief of staff, Major General Andrew Humphreys, "expressed himself displeased with the clumsiness of the Deep Bottom 'surprise.'" As a result of this unrecorded consultation, Grant decided to pull Mott's Division from the north side of the James that evening. With his energy now fully devoted to the mine attack at Petersburg, the commander in chief kept the remainder of the expeditionary force in place, hoping that Hancock's presence would cause Lee to rush reinforcements north and further weaken his force at Petersburg. Hancock would remain until the following evening, July 29, and then return to Petersburg to support Burnside's attack.[186]

Hancock's chain of command was disrupted when Barlow received the crushing news that his wife, Arabella, had died from typhus the previous day. Arabella had been serving as a nurse at City Point when she fell ill and traveled to Washington, D.C., to recover. She quickly deteriorated and died on July 27. Barlow was "entirely incapacitated by this sudden grief" and was "driven…insane." At first Meade refused to let Barlow leave, since he was in the middle of an active operation, but the crusty curmudgeon eventually relented and granted the stricken general a leave of absence. Nelson Miles would take command of the First Division.[187]

Mott's men had been working hard all day reversing the Confederate trenches that they had occupied when word came down from headquarters at 7:30 p.m. to cease all activity and wait until cover of darkness to move to the lower pontoon bridge. Hancock requested that Butler's troops build small fires along the road so that Mott's men could see on their way back across the pontoon bridge. At 9:00 p.m., Mott's soldiers crossed the James and trudged all night long, crossing the Appomattox at Point of Rocks. One soldier in Mott's Division recalled that "[t]he march was rapid and fatiguing," while John Haley, avoiding the provost guard this time, recorded in his journal:

About 9 o'clock in the evening we started on a movement, whither or wherefore we knew not. We hadn't gone far when we discovered a deucedly familiar look to the area. We soon arrived at, and crossed, the James, then followed a southeast course to the Appomattox...The night was spent marching...We suffered from heat, thirst, and infinite dust.

Foster could see Mott's men withdrawing and thought that it was the entire II Corps going back. He frantically sent word to X Corps headquarters that he was being abandoned and that he feared a Confederate attack in the morning that would "result in a disaster to my command" and send the Union gunboats packing. General Birney responded that all was well, although it is doubtful that Foster got much sleep that night.[188]

Back at City Point, a surprisingly optimistic Grant sent a telegram to Washington, D.C., informing Chief of Staff Halleck about the days' events. He admitted, "We have failed in what I had hoped to accomplish—that is, to surprise the enemy, and get on to their roads with the cavalry near to Richmond and destroy them out to [the] South Anna." If there was any glimmer of hope, it was now to be found at Petersburg and at Petersburg alone—the mine attack must succeed. The force left at Deep Bottom was the key to siphoning off men from Lee's army to ensure that success. With that in mind, Grant concluded, "I am yet in hopes of turning this diversion to account, so as to yield greater results than if the first object had been accomplished."[189]

"Gen. Lee Seems to Have Considered This Movement of Hancock's a Very Dangerous One"

While Mott's men were making their way back to Petersburg, Lee was preparing reinforcements to send in the opposite direction. At 9:00 p.m., he sent Fitzhugh Lee's and W.H.F. "Rooney" Lee's battle-hardened cavalry troopers north with orders to report to General Anderson. "Fitz" Lee received these orders at 9:30 p.m. and was en route shortly after midnight. Major General Charles W. Field's division left its trenches around Petersburg that evening and marched all night, arriving north of the James in the early morning hours of July 29.[190]

While Lee himself did not deem it important enough to leave Petersburg for the front, he did want to make sure that the next attack would have a key element that had been lacking the past two days: proper artillery support. Lee thus met with his artillery chief, Brigadier General William Nelson Pendleton, and told him to make sure that Anderson had everything he needed. After meeting with Lee, Pendleton wrote to his wife:

> *My idea is that Grant does not intend a bona fide attempt on Richmond at this juncture; but as he has, by means of his pontoon-bridge near Bermuda Hundred, defended by his gunboats, a shorter line to and fro than we have via Drewry's Bluff, he will try to draw General Lee over there, and then suddenly recross all his force to the neighborhood of Petersburg, and make a concentrated attack either on the line near the town or on that across the Peninsula between the James and the Appomattox.*[191]

The Confederate buildup was immense, and it showed that Lee was still willing to gamble—as Edward Porter Alexander later said, "Gen. Lee seems to have considered this movement of Hancock's a very dangerous one," since this massive Confederate concentration "left in all the Petersburg lines only three divisions of infantry, Hoke's, Johnson's, & Mahone's, instead of the seven which usually garrisoned them."[192]

When all of these reinforcements were in place on the north side of the James, Anderson planned to launch an overwhelming attack that would crush Hancock and Sheridan's men and destroy once and for all the Deep Bottom bridgehead.

Chapter 8

July 29, 1864

"Questions Equally Hard to Answer"

In the early morning hours of July 29, Hancock devised a desperate scheme to convince the Confederates that he was still being reinforced rather than having troops taken away from his command. To pull this off, he had portions of Torbert's Division ride to the south side of the James River. The troopers were ordered to leave their horses at Bermuda Hundred and wait until the sun had risen. Then, making sure that they were within easy eyesight of the Confederates, they were to march back over the bridge and rejoin Hancock, giving the impression that they were infantry reinforcements.[193]

Torbert's exhausted cavalrymen rode to the pontoon bridge at 1:00 a.m. At the bridge, the cavalry met Mott's Division, which was also crossing, and "the compliments, usual when cavalry and infantry meet in a crowded road, passed between the two columns." When the men finally did begin to cross, they found the bridge once again covered with hay "to prevent the tramp of the horses from being heard." At 3:30 a.m., the head of Torbert's column reached the camps on Jones' Neck and dropped off the horses. As the sun began to rise, Torbert's cavalry recrossed the bridge. As a soldier in the 1st Pennsylvania Reserve Cavalry noted, "At nine, A.M....the regiment again crossed to the north side of the James, and threw up rifle pits in front of the brigade...we occupying nearly the same position held by us on the 27th."[194]

One Confederate who was thoroughly confused by Sheridan's trick was Richard S. Ewell. "Old Bald Head" confided to his wife in a private letter that he could not comprehend these movements at all: "Why did Sheridan cross or why did he go back, or whether he went back or if he did not go back, where is he, are questions equally hard to answer." Hancock, no doubt, would have been pleased to know how effective this ruse was to such a high-ranking Confederate officer.[195]

Back at City Point, Grant was concerned with reinforcements wearing a different-colored uniform. He tasked George H. Sharpe of the Bureau of Military Information to question some deserters who had recently come into Federal lines. From them, Sharpe learned that "brigades from three different Confederate divisions had departed Petersburg and moved north." This news prompted Grant to write to Meade, "The enemy are evidently piling everything...to the north side of the river...I am inclined to think the enemy will wait for us to attack, unless they discover that we are withdrawing." Armed with this knowledge, Grant and Meade devoted most of their attention to Burnside's mine attack for the remainder of the day.[196]

Hancock now had 14,437 men left whom Mott had returned to Petersburg. He positioned them in a compact formation near the bridgehead so that the gunboats could fire over the heads of his men. As usual, Hancock fretted over his dispositions. As a member of his staff later wrote:

> *His position on the 29th was therefore to be one of great peril. His line possessed no natural advantages whatever and the troops he had left with him were but a fraction of what would have been required to hold it against a serious attack. To draw in that line would have been to invite a movement of the enemy, which could hardly have failed to disclose Hancock's weakness. Were the enemy even to suspect that weakness, they would pour down in overwhelming force and drive our troops into the river.*[197]

Meanwhile, Anderson's Confederates remained idle. The lieutenant general moved back to Riddell's Shop, with plans to renew the battle, when it was discovered that Hancock had retired to New Market Road. Anderson later reported:

> *The position of the enemy was reconnoitered on the following morning and he was found to be occupying a line running from Deep Bottom, by Sweeney*

Pottery, to the junction of the Darbytown and Long Bridge Roads and thence down the Long Bridge Road beyond Darby's House and breaking off from that point in the direction of Malvern Hill.

With Field's infantry and the cavalry of Fitzhugh and Rooney Lee en route, Anderson decided to launch a large-scale attack on the morning of July 30.[198] In the meantime, Anderson attempted to seize the juncture of Darbytown and Long Bridge Roads for the larger attack to come on the thirtieth. According to Anderson, "Conner's and Kershaw's Brigades were moved to the vicinity of the junction of the Darbytown and Long Bridge Roads, W.H.F. Lee's Cavalry covering our left."[199]

In the interim, a unique occurrence took place in the camps of the North Carolina troops: the men got to vote for governor of the Old North State. The election pitted the sitting governor, Zebulon Vance, against William W. Holden of the controversial Peace Party. Holden's party was dedicated to suing for peace with the Federal government. This was not done out of any sort of pro-Union or antislavery sentiment—rather, the Peace Party viewed negotiating with the North as the only viable alternative left for establishing an Independent South.

James Harris of the 7th North Carolina reported that "in the 7th regiment Governor Vance received 94 votes and W.W. Holden, Esq. 23." Colonel William H.A. Speer, who commanded the 28th North Carolina, felt the need to write to Governor Vance himself to report his victory:

I have the honor & pleasure of writing that my Regt. voted as follows: Vance 179, Holden 31. This vote is after a hard day's fight in which I have lost near 100 men. We had a river engagement with the cavalry. I am certain your election is certain, which I am very proud of...If it had not been for the fight, your vote would have been much larger. I think I have done well, as several of my company are from Holden's counties.

Another Tarheel reminisced that "[t]he contest in North Carolina was a warm one, but in our regiment it was all one way." It was reported that Vance beat Holden by eleven thousand votes in the Army of Northern Virginia.[200]

Not everyone was pleased with the results, as evidenced by a telegram sent from Hancock on the morning of the twenty-ninth. Hancock informed Chief of Staff Humphreys about two deserters from Heth's Division who came into Union lines that morning. "They deserted," said Hancock, "because they were not allowed to vote...They say that in very few cases...

were any allowed to vote who did not vote for Vance." These deserters were illustrative of a wave of desertion that followed the 1864 gubernatorial race in North Carolina.[201]

"YANKEES, FLIES & OTHER VERMIN"

As temperatures rose to a scorching ninety-eight degrees that afternoon, Anderson was ready to move his men toward Riddell's Shop at the intersection of Charles City and Darbytown Roads. Kershaw launched an infantry assault from Fussell's Mill, while cavalry under Gary and Rooney Lee moved down Charles City Road from Deep Run toward Riddell's Shop.[202]

Around 5:00 p.m., the 9th Virginia Cavalry of Chambliss's Brigade arrived at Malvern Hill and ran off the pickets of the 1st Maine Cavalry. The Confederates initially forced the Federals back in what one trooper called "a spirited action with the enemy on the classic field at Malvern Hill." The 9th lost about fifteen men and a few horses before being pushed back by its Federal counterparts. When the fighting was done, Sergeant Rawleigh Dunaway of the 9th Virginia complained that he was sick of fighting "Yankees, flies & other vermin."[203]

While the cavalry was busily engaged, Kershaw's men tangled with the Federal pickets who had been left along the Long Bridge Road the previous day. During this fight, twenty-year-old lieutenant Arthur G. Sedgwick—the nephew of the VI Corps commander killed at Spotsylvania Court House—and a detail of thirty men he was leading were gobbled up and humiliatingly marched through the streets of Richmond. According to the *Richmond Daily Dispatch*, "[F]ifteen [prisoners] were Germans, and from them we learn that there were three hundred foreigners in the 20th Massachusetts who were regularly enlisted in the Yankee service before leaving Germany for the United States." Sedgwick was sent to Libby Prison, where he sat out the remainder of the war.[204]

With the day's skirmishing concluded, Anderson's long-awaited reinforcements began to pour into his lines. Field's men "took cars on the morning of the 29th on the Petersburg and Richmond Railroad for Rice's Station." From there, the men marched across the James at Drewry's Bluff and pushed on to Fussell's Mill. The march was especially difficult for the men, with one exhausted soldier noting, "[R]oads dusty and sun dreadful warm—great many men give out."[205]

Fitzhugh Lee's men pushed through the awful conditions to reach the north side of the James as well. As Major James D. Ferguson, Lee's assistant adjutant general, wrote in his memorandum book:

> *Passed through Petersburg before daylight…resumed the march at 9 o'clock, crossed the pontoon bridge at Drewry's Bluff…moved Lomax's to Laurel Hill Church on New Market Road, where it is encamped—we made Headquarters there. Kershaw's Brigade reported engaged with the enemy yesterday and was worsted. Distance marched since last night, thirty miles.*[206]

With every gray-clad soldier who set foot on the north side of the James, Burnside's chances of success grew greater and greater—as did the anxiety level of Winfield Scott Hancock.

"I Will Hold You Responsible for Your Line and Everything That May Happen Here"

Hancock was so beside himself that he fearfully checked and rechecked the dispositions of his men during the morning hours. While conducting this inspection, he came across what he considered to be a glaring error in Gibbon's sector, prompting him to ride up to the hapless general and berate him for the second time in less than twenty-four hours. Gibbon was sitting with Sheridan and several other high-ranking officers when Hancock rode up and bawled, "Is General Gibbon here?"

Gibbon stood up only to be cursed out by Hancock, who demanded to know what halfwit had laid out his line. When Gibbon confessed that he had laid out his own lines, an irate Hancock exclaimed for all to hear, "Get on your horse, and come with me. I will show you where it is defective!"

After a short ride, Gibbon and Hancock arrived at the disputed point, where the corps commander schooled his subordinate about a point in the lines where he thought that the Confederates could advance unseen by the nearby infantry. Gibbon calmly pointed out that there were cannons nearby that could decimate any Rebels who penetrated this sector, stating, "I give the enemy odds if he will attack here for he will be defeated."

It was clear that Hancock had not seen this battery in his first pass through this area. Stammering, the general replied, "Well, I will hold you responsible for your line and everything that may happen here."

Gibbon shot back, "General, I am perfectly willing to be so held responsible and I regret you had not come to that conclusion before insulting me in such a way before half a dozen general officers of the army."

A defeated Hancock apologized and stated that he would also extend an apology to the officers who had heard him disparage Gibbon in such a vicious manner. This incident marked the end of Gibbon and Hancock's friendship and led to the affronted officer seeking a transfer to a different command.[207]

Hancock's mood did not improve when he was informed of the skirmishing with Kershaw's men at about 5:30 p.m. When it was clear that he was not going to be overrun, Hancock issued a circular command:

> *The command will commence withdrawing at early dark, as follows: The Cavalry Corps, under direction of Major-General Sheridan, by the lower pontoon bridge…The Second Corps will commence withdrawing at early dark, the Second Division leading, crossing the upper pontoon bridge, keeping to the right of the road in all cases, taking the road to Point of Rocks, crossing the Appomattox at that place…The brigade (General Birge's) of the Nineteenth Corps will follow the First Division to the bridge-head, where it will take position, holding the tete-de-pont. The pickets will be withdrawn at dark to the line of intrenchments held by the infantry, and General Sheridan will establish a line of pickets connecting the right of this line with the rear. As soon as the brigade of the Nineteenth Corps is in position in the tete-de-pont General Birge will relieve the picket line of the Second Corps from the intrenchments. As soon as General Sheridan's new picket line is withdrawn General Birge can establish such picket line as he may think proper for the defense of his position…The train of the Second Corps…will move at dark to the park of the general corps train beyond the Appomattox…Every exertion must be made to prevent this train obstructing the march of troops.[208]*

One can only imagine the sense of relief Hancock experienced knowing that he was finally extricating himself from the north side of the James River.

"My Command Is Now Across the Bridge"

As darkness began to fall, Hancock requested that Butler light fires along the roadways yet again. The general exhaled a sigh of relief when the reply came back, "The road is lighted. An officer is stationed at the neck at the first fire who will direct the column." After sunset, Gibbon's Division moved out at 7:30 p.m., followed by Miles's men. By 11:20 p.m., Hancock was able to wire Meade, "My command is now across the bridge."[209]

Once again, the experience of a night march was nightmarish for the weary foot soldiers. A soldier in the 36th Wisconsin described a "great many of the brigade staying out and falling behind. About two o'clock I fell out and crawled into a fallen tree top and rested until it began to be daylight." It was another "hard march on which many straggled," wrote the surgeon of the 19th Massachusetts. Birge's troops were the last men to step off the shore of the north bank of the James.[210]

With the Union lines being bolstered with the return of Hancock's men and the Rebel trenches surrounding Petersburg depleted of men, the stage was set for one of the great Union victories of the war.

Chapter 9

CLOSING SCENES

"IT DEGENERATES INTO *MURDER*"

As the sun rose on the morning of July 30, Hancock's two divisions filed wearily into the lines at Petersburg. Jonah Dyer of the 19th Massachusetts recalled how Gibbon's men staggered into the lines "after a hard march on which many straggled, and reached our works in front of Petersburg at daylight." Private John Ryan of the 28th Massachusetts complained, "We had been marching hard all night, and were tired, sleepy, and dusty." What they witnessed next no doubt woke many of them up.[211]

At 4:44 a.m., eight thousand pounds of gunpowder blasted a massive hole in the Confederate works at Elliott's Salient. Private Haley complained that "our slumbers were terminated as abruptly as though Gabriel himself had tooted his horn in our ears." Father William Corby of the Irish Brigade was awed by what he saw:

> We witnessed from some distance the destructive work of death. A great mass of earth was lifted, with a sudden electric force, carrying heavenward with it batteries, men, timber…until, reaching a certain height, it spread out like a cloud, and then all came crashing down in horrid confusion.

Haley concluded, "The Union loss in this affair is frightful, and when we consider the paltry results, it degenerates into *murder*."[212]

While the Battle of the Crater developed, Mott's beleaguered men were ordered out in a skirmish line to probe the Confederate works in their front. General Meade informed Hancock at 7:00 a.m., "If Burnside…gain[s] the crest the enemy cannot hold it in your front, for they will be open to attack from front and rear…If you have reason to believe that their condition is such that an effort to dislodge them would be successful I would like to have it made." Two hours later, he was ordered to stand down and "hold in force." Many a Cloverleaf was no doubt relieved to be spared from participating in this attack, although Private Herbert Willand did lament that "the fort would have been held and the result altogether different" if the II Corps had made the attack.[213]

For many of the men who had participated in the First Deep Bottom Campaign, the Battle of the Crater marked a painful climax to an already perplexing series of events. John D. Timmerman of the 3rd New York Cavalry confessed, "[I]t is the first time that I have been on a raid of any kind that I did not form Some idea of what was going on, and I am somewhat puzzled to know…but I suppose I will have to wait for the papers to tell me." Private Daniel A. Britton of the 36th Wisconsin was much gloomier when he wrote to his wife on August 2: "I suppose the news will go north that it was a great victory. I cant cal it much of a victory. I have come to the conclusion that this war wil never be settled by fighting they have got to come to some other way of settlement."[214]

"Lee Is the Master of the Situation"

In the Confederate camps, Anderson stirred his men and had Field's fresh troops move down the Long Bridge Road and deploy skirmishers. The cavalry was ordered to move out as well. Major James D. Ferguson, assistant adjutant general to Fitzhugh Lee, wrote in his memorandum book that he had been ordered "to Fussell's Mill on the Darbytown Road and went to the same place." Anderson was chagrined to find that his grand battle plan for the day was now irrelevant, for "it was discovered that the enemy had retired and recrossed the river leaving some force in their entrenchments at Deep Bottom."[215]

After a brief encounter with some Union cavalry nearby, the Confederates entered a Yankee camp that had just been abandoned. A famished Confederate was filled with disbelief at what the Federals had left behind:

"They had left almost everything. They had tried to destroy their plunder. They had cut up their blankets and clothes, and had left their breakfast on the fire. Some had potatoes, some chicken and butter, all of which they had taken from the citizens—to which our boys done full justice." The men wandered around, replenishing their skinny haversacks until the nearby gunboats lobbed a few shells at them and encouraged them to retire to their previous positions.

In Richmond, John B. Jones was relieved that he and his fellow clerks had not been called out to deal with the Federal incursion at Deep Bottom, as Ewell had repeatedly requested. He wrote in his diary:

> *The enemy has mostly countermarched from this side of the river...and rumor says there are little or no forces of either party on the north side of the James this morning. This was probably Grant's grand stratagem for our destruction, and it has failed disastrously for him. What will he do next? No matter what, Lee is the master of the situation.*[216]

In reality, determining who was truly the master of the situation was much more ambiguous.

Ulysses S. Grant gave scant attention to the First Deep Bottom Campaign in his memoirs. Other than boasting, "We were successful in drawing the enemy's troops to the north side of the James as I expected," Grant did not delve deeply into his grand strategy for the campaign. Perhaps that was because it was unclear from the very start. The campaign was birthed more from political considerations, and the commander in chief did not spend much time in the way of preparation before heaving an expeditionary force north of the James. Furthermore, once the expedition was launched, Grant spent little time at the front and was occupied more with the mine assault than what was happening with Hancock and Sheridan. By the twenty-eighth, he was content to leave the force in place to siphon off troops from Lee's army and leave it at that. He clearly did not learn from his missteps, as an identical expedition north of the James was launched less than a month later.[217]

There is little in the performance of Winfield Scott Hancock that merits praise. Beginning with the decision to cross his entire force at the lower pontoon bridge, thus irrevocably altering the nature of the plan, the corps commander's performance did not improve measurably. After a successful assault on Tilghman's Gate, Hancock seems to have succumbed to the movement of phantom brigades and wasted an entire day. When Anderson's counterattack was launched on July 28, all hopes for any aggressive movement were lost; the timid general was content to hunker down near the bridgehead and let events play themselves out. The physical pain of his Gettysburg wound combined with the mental strain of uninterrupted service since the start of the Overhand Campaign. Hancock's failure showed that he had reached his core level of competence at the corps level and was not suitable for independent command.

Phil Sheridan gave an astonishingly hands-off performance, contenting himself to follow Hancock's orders and have his subordinates execute them. In later years, Sheridan tried to explain this away with the duplicitous comment, "In the expedition to Deep Bottom I was under the command of Major-General Hancock, who, by seniority, was to control my corps as well as his own until the way was opened up for me to get out on the Virginia Central railroad." In a remarkable turn of events, the cavalry turned in the best performance of all on the Union side, and none of the credit was due to its commander.[218]

For Robert E. Lee, the First Deep Bottom Campaign was frustrating from start to finish. Some of this frustration was of his own making, since he was primarily responsible for the confusion over just who was in charge of what on the north side of the river. The situation was out of his control by July 28, as evidenced by his heated messages to Ewell inquiring who was in charge and what was taking place.

Lee's top subordinate, Richard Anderson, failed his commanding general. He was unable to get all of the troops he had brought with him into the battle, thus setting up his humiliating defeat at the Darby Farm. Heth's men contributed nothing of consequence on July 28, and three of Kershaw's four brigades were left behind as well. When the attack was launched, there was no reconnaissance, and Anderson apparently did not even think to bring in artillery support for his men.

Ewell's performance was hampered by the ambiguous command structure, which left him in more of a supporting than active role throughout the campaign. Although his mandate as the leader of the Department of Richmond was to protect the city from any Federal threats, the waters became muddied once soldiers from the Army of Northern Virginia showed up with the same mission. Ewell tried to explain his role in a letter to his wife on July 29: "This is an amount of philosophy you wont credit me for, but I am chiefly in charge of the defense of Richmond. The movements of troops in the field are to a great degree directed by Genl Anderson under Genl Lee, it being a mixed sort of concern."[219]

First Deep Bottom marked Joseph B. Kershaw's worst performance of the war. His absence on the morning of July 27 led to the capture of Tilghman's Gate and the loss of Graham's four Parrott guns. Like Hancock, General Kershaw proved that he was incapable of independent command.

All told, Hancock's command lost 62 killed, 340 wounded and 86 missing, for a grand total of 488 casualties. The Confederates lost 471 killed and wounded and another 208 captured, for a total of 679 casualties.[220]

The main positive contribution of the First Deep Bottom Campaign was its success at drawing off Confederates in front of Petersburg. As E.P. Alexander wryly put it, the Federals left "our 6 divisions at Deep Bottom with their thumbs to suck." Noted historian Richard J. Sommers posited, "It is all the more significant because it was the first of a series of battles that characterized the operations of Grant and Lee for the rest of 1864 and in many respects for the rest of the Siege of Petersburg."[221]

Grant's strategy of sending a force north of the James while simultaneously threatening Petersburg would not bear much fruit until the end of September 1864, when he was finally able to gain a toehold north of the James during the Battle of Chaffin's Farm. When Richmond fell in April 1865, Union troops marched forth from the fortifications captured during this battle to occupy the Confederate capital.

As time passed, the story of the Richmond-Petersburg Campaign became a confusing tangle of troop movements across fields less picturesque than Gettysburg and Antietam. Battles like First Deep Bottom were relegated to the dustbin of history for all except men like Ben Naylor and his counterparts in gray.

With an intervening span of 150 years since these events occurred, smaller actions such as First Deep Bottom cry out for scholars to chronicle them and tell the stories of the men who were caught up in a tide of events much larger than they could have ever comprehended.

Who will write up those fights?

NOTES

Chapter 1

1. Nevins, *War for the Union*, 49; Early, *Campaigns of Gen. Robert E. Lee*, 37.
2. Nicolay and Hay, *Abraham Lincoln*, 563.
3. Basler, *Collected Works of Abraham Lincoln*, 395–96.
4. Mackey, *Documentary History of the Civil War Era*, 135.
5. Simon, *Papers of Ulysses S. Grant*, 191; Basler, *Collected Works of Abraham Lincoln*, 451.

Chapter 2

6. Weld, *War Diary and Letters of Stephen Minot Weld*, 213.
7. John C. Ropes, "Grant's Campaign in Virginia in 1864," in *Papers of the Military Historical Society of Massachusetts*, 402–3.
8. Fox, *Regimental Losses in the American Civil War*, 69.
9. Walker, *History of the Second Army Corps*, 512.
10. Quoted in Kreiser, *Defeating Lee*, 199; Walker, *History of the Second Army Corps*, 544.
11. Quoted in Styple, *Generals in Bronze*, 75; *Military Order of the Loyal Legion*, 32.
12. Samito, *"Fear Was Not in Him,"* xvi–xx.
13. Kreiser, *Defeating Lee*, 155; Samito, *"Fear Was Not in Him,"* 199, 205.
14. Agassiz, *Meade's Headquarters*, 107.
15. Warner, *Generals in Blue*, 171–72.
16. *New York Times*, "General Mott's Sudden Death," November 30, 1864.

17. Warner, *Generals in Blue*, 338.

18. James I. Robertson Jr., "Diary of a Southern Refugee during the War, June 1863–July 1864," in Davis and Robertson, *Virginia at War, 1864*, 189.

19. Sheehan-Dean, *Why Confederates Fought*, 164.

20. Young, *Lee's Army during the Overland Campaign*, 213–32; quoted in Power, *Lee's Miserables*, 2; quoted in Gallagher, *Confederate War*, 44–45.

21. Quoted in Dufour, *Nine Men in Gray*, 190.

22. Jones, *Campbell Brown's Civil War*, 267.

23. Walker, *Life of Lieutenant General Richard Heron Anderson*, 263.

24. Warner, *Generals in Gray*, 171.

25. Ibid., 145; William Alan Blair, "Benjamin Grubb Humphreys," in Davis, *Confederate General*, 133.

26. Warner, *Generals in Gray*, 102; Holland, *24th Virginia Cavalry*, 78.

Chapter 3

27. Sumner, *Diary of Cyrus Comstock*, 274.

28. Porter, *Campaigning with Grant*, 216.

29. *War of the Rebellion: A Compilation of the Official Records of the Union and Confederate Armies*, vol. 40, pt. 2, 222 (hereafter *OR*).

30. Ibid., vol. 40, pt. 2, 213–14.

31. Ibid., vol. 40, pt. 2, 262.

32. Ibid., vol. 40, pt. 2, 263, 298.

33. Samuel H. Root Memoir, Civil War Miscellaneous Collection, U.S. Army Heritage and Education Center; Dickey, *History of the Eighty-fifth Pennsylvania Volunteer Infantry*, 339; Roe, Amory, Cook and Hill, *Twenty-fourth Regiment Massachusetts Volunteers*, 319.

34. *OR*, vol. 40, pt. 1, 677.

35. Ibid.; Maxfield and Brady, *Company D, Eleventh Maine*, 36.

36. Stowits, *History of the One Hundredth Regiment*, 272–73; *OR*, vol. 40, pt. 1, 677; Wixson, *Echoes from the Boys*, 350.

37. *OR*, vol. 40, pt. 2, 297.

38. Ibid., vol. 40, pt. 2, 673.

39. Pfanz, *Richard S. Ewell*, 405; *OR*, vol. 40, pt. 2, 673; *OR*, vol. 51, pt. 2, 1,082.

40. *OR*, vol. 40, pt. 2, 297; Dickey, *History of the Eighty-fifth Pennsylvania Volunteer Infantry*, 339.

41. *OR*, vol. 51, pt. 2, 1,026.

42. Driver, *1ˢᵗ and 2ⁿᵈ Rockbridge Artillery*, 50.

43. *Official Records of the Union and Confederate Navies in the War of the Rebellion*, vol. 10, 225–26 (hereafter *ORN*); Suderow, "War Along the James," 14.

44. Quoted in Naval History Division, *Civil War Navy Chronology*, iv–83; Lake and Cooper, *I Take My Pen in Hand*, 124.

45. *OR*, vol. 40, pt. 3, 745.

46. Stowits, *History of the One Hundredth Regiment*, 216; Caldwell, *History of a Brigade of South Carolinians*, 168.

47. *OR*, vol. 40, pt. 3, 764; Suderow, "War Along the James," 15.

48. *OR*, vol. 40, pt. 3, 745; Maxfield and Brady, *Company D, Eleventh Maine*, 38.

49. W.H. Merriam, "Grant! Affairs on the James River," *New York Herald*, July 19, 1864.

50. *OR*, vol. 40, pt. 3, 377.

51. Maxfield and Brady, *Company D, Eleventh Maine*, 38; *OR*, vol. 40, pt. 3, 383, 419.

52. *OR*, vol. 40, pt. 2, 599.

53. Dowdey and Manarin, *Wartime Papers of Robert E. Lee*, 825.

54. *OR*, vol. 40, pt. 3, 795–96.

55. Ibid.; Paul Agulus McMichael Diary, South Caroliniana Library, University South Caroliniana Society Manuscripts Collections, University of South Carolina; *OR*, vol. 40, pt. 1, 695; *Story of One Regiment*, 224.

56. *OR*, vol. 40, pt. 1, 695.

57. James Martin to Sister, August 3, 1864, Martin Letter Collection, South Carolina Confederate Relic Room and Military Museum; Beecher, *History of the First Light Battery*, 518.

58. Maxfield and Brady, *Company D, Eleventh Maine*, 39.

59. Long, *Personal Memoirs of U.S. Grant*, 465.

60. Ibid.

61. *OR*, vol. 40, pt. 3, 437.

62. Ibid.

63. Ibid., vol. 40, pt. 3, 438.

64. Ibid., vol. 40, pt. 3, 464.

65. Ibid., vol. 40, pt. 3, 465–66.

66. Cavanaugh and Marvel, *Battle of the Crater*, 28.

67. Silliker, *Rebel Yell & the Yankee Hurrah*, 184.

68. C.A.P., "The Operations of Wednesday," *New York Tribune*, August 1, 1864.

69. Suderow, "Glory Denied," 21.

70. *Supplement to the Official Records*, pt. 1, vol. 7, 245 (hereafter *OR Supplement*).

71. *OR*, vol. 40, pt. 1, 309.

72. Ibid., vol. 40, pt. 3, 509–10.

73. Walker, *History of the Second Army Corps*, 560.

74. Stevens, *Berdan's United States Sharpshooters*, 473.

75. White, *Civil War Diary of Wyman S. White*, 143.

76. *OR*, vol. 40, pt. 3, 510.

Chapter 4

77. *OR*, vol. 40, pt. 1, 389; Silliker, *Rebel Yell & the Yankee Hurrah*, 184.

78. *OR*, vol. 40, pt. 1, 800; Humphreys to Kershaw, July 30, 1864, in Benjamin Grubb Humphreys Papers, Mississippi Department of Archives and History; Sturkey, *Hampton Legion Infantry*, 84.

79. *OR*, vol. 40, pt. 1, 331, 374, 379; De Trobriand, *Four Years with the Army of the Potomac*, 606.

80. Dyer, *Journal of a Civil War Surgeon*, 181.

81. De Trobriand, *Four Years with the Army of the Potomac*, 606.

82. Trumbull, *Knightly Soldier*, 256.

83. Barnard, *Campaigning with the Irish Brigade*, 120; Dyer, *Journal of a Civil War Surgeon*, 181.

84. Trumbull, *Knightly Soldier*, 256.

85. De Trobriand, *Four Years with the Army of the Potomac*, 606.

86. Humphreys to Kershaw, July 30, 1864; C.A., *Daily Richmond Examiner*, August 1, 1864.

87. Rawlinson, *Walter Stewart Family History*, 425.

88. *Daily Richmond Examiner*, July 29, 1864, and August 1, 1864.

89. Trumbull, *Knightly Soldier*, 258; Barnard, *Campaigning with the Irish Brigade*, 121.

90. Rhodes, *History of Battery B*, 310; Humphreys to Kershaw, July 30, 1864.

91. George Gove to Julia Parsons, August 2, 1864, Box 2, Folder 19, Parsons Family Papers, Milne Special Collections and Archives, University of New Hampshire; quoted in Driver, *1ˢᵗ and 2ⁿᵈ Rockbridge Artillery*, 50; *Daily Richmond Examiner*, August 1, 1864; White, "Diary of the War," 267.

92. *OR*, vol. 40, pt. 1, 696; Barnard, *Campaigning with the Irish Brigade*, 122; Silliker, *Rebel Yell & the Yankee Hurrah*, 185; *New York Herald*, "Mr. Finley Anderson's Dispatch," July 30, 1864.

93. Billings, *History of the Tenth Massachusetts*, 296.

94. Humphreys to Kershaw, July 30, 1864.

95. *Daily Richmond Examiner*, July 29, 1864.

96. Humphreys to Kershaw, July 30, 1864; *OR*, vol. 40, pt. 1, 241–44; Silliker, *Rebel Yell & the Yankee Hurrah*, 185.

97. Crosland, *Reminiscences of the Sixties*, 27.

98. Suderow, "Glory Denied," 22.

99. Crosland, *Reminiscences of the Sixties*, 27.

100. Ibid.

101. *OR*, vol. 40, pt. 1, 409; De Trobriand, *Four Years with the Army of the Potomac*, 606; Crosland, *Reminiscences of the Sixties*, 27.

102. Compiled Service Records, Benjamin E. Nicholson, Hampton Legion, NARA RG 109; William T. Walton, "A History of Scenes Around Richmond, 1864," *Recollections and Reminiscences 1861–1865*, 42.

103. C.M. Maull, "An Incident of the Late War," *Sunny South*, August 29, 1896.

104. Theophilus G. Barham, "War Record of T.G. Barham," 31.

105. Crosland, *Reminiscences of the Sixties*, 27; West, *Found Among the Privates*, 72–73.

106. Ibid.

107. Crosland, *Reminiscences of the Sixties*, 27; Barham, "War Record of T.G. Barham," 31.

108. *Story of One Regiment*, 229.

109. Sumner, *Diary of Cyrus Comstock*, 284.

110. Porter, *Campaigning with Grant*, 259–60.

111. *OR*, vol. 40, pt. 1, 322.

112. Ibid., vol. 40, pt. 3, 810–11; Suderow, "Glory Denied," 26.

113. *OR*, vol. 40, pt. 3, 807–9; Jones, *Rebel War Clerk's Diary*, 256.

114. Walker, *History of the Second Army Corps*, 563; *OR*, vol. 40, pt. 3, 502.

Chapter 5

115. *OR*, vol. 40, pt. 3, 544–45.

116. Ibid., vol. 40, pt. 3, 545–46.

117. Ibid., vol. 40, pt. 1, 374, 379.

118. Ibid., vol. 40, pt. 3, 516–17.

119. *New York Daily Tribune*, July 30, 1864; *OR*, vol. 40, pt. 1, 426.

120. *OR*, vol. 40, pt. 1, 180; Walker, *History of the Second Army Corps*, 564; Barnard, *Campaigning with the Irish Brigade*, 122.

121. *OR*, vol. 40, pt. 1, 309–10.

122. Ibid., vol. 40, pt. 1, 331, 388–89.

123. Lieutenant Frank M. Kelley to Mother, July 28, 1864, quoted in *Blue & Gray* 30, no. 5 (2014): 85.

124. *OR*, vol. 40, pt. 3, 512.

125. Ibid., vol. 40, pt. 3, 512–13.

126. Rodenbough, *From Everglade to Canon*, 331; Sheridan, *Personal Memoirs*, 447; *New York Tribune*, "The Operations of Wednesday," August 1, 1864.

127. *OR*, vol. 40, pt. 3, 513.

128. Ibid., vol. 40, pt. 3, 514, 532.

129. Ibid., vol. 40, pt. 3, 505, 515, 536.

130. Ibid., vol. 40, pt. 3, 504.

131. Ibid., vol. 40, pt. 3, 502.

132. Ibid., vol. 40, pt. 3, 322, 389, 392.

133. Ware, "Enroughty, Darby and General McClellan"; see also Green, *Word Book of Virginia*, 14.

134. Dowdey and Manarin, *Wartime Papers of Robert E. Lee*, 826.

135. *OR Supplement*, vol. 7, 252.

136. *OR Supplement*, vol. 7, 332; James William Thomas Diary, Dielman Collection, MDHS.

Chapter 6

137. Krick, *Civil War Weather in Virginia*, 134; *OR*, vol. 40, pt. 3, 560.

138. *OR*, vol. 40, pt. 3, 560, 552.

139. Ibid., vol. 40, pt. 3, 585–86.

140. Ibid., vol. 40, pt. 1, 619.

141. Ibid., vol. 40, pt. 3, 813.

142. Caldwell, *History of a Brigade of South Carolinians*, 170.

143. Report of Major J.S. Bost, August 3, 1864, James H. Lane Papers, Series 1, Box 2, Folder 74, Auburn University Special Collections & Archives Department; Caldwell, *History of a Brigade of South Carolinians*, 170.

144. Caldwell, *History of a Brigade of South Carolinians*, 170.

145. Nathan B. Webb Diaries, Schoff Civil War Collection, Clements Library, University of Michigan, 12–13.

146. Caldwell, *History of a Brigade of South Carolinians*, 170–71; Hagemann, *Fighting Rebels and Redskins*, 252–53; Foster, *Reminiscences and Record of the 6th New York*, 85.

147. Harris, *Historical Sketches of the Seventh Regiment*, 53.

148. Report of Lieutenant Colonel W.H.A. Speer, James H. Lane Papers, Series 1, Box 2, Folder 74, Auburn University Special Collections & Archives Department.

149. Report of Major J.S. Bost, Lane Papers.

150. Cheney, *History of the Ninth Regiment*, 199–200; Taylor, *Saddle and Saber*, 167.

151. Caldwell, *History of a Brigade of South Carolinians*, 171.

152. Callais Report, Lane Papers.

153. Cheney, *History of the Ninth Regiment*, 200; E.A. Paul, *New York Times*, August 11, 1864.

154. A.E. Shore to E.H. and [?] Shore, Chafins [*sic*] Bluff, August 2, 1864, Augustin E. Shore correspondence, Manuscript, Archives and Rare Book Library, Emory University; Report of Captain J.G. Harris, July 29, 1864, James H. Lane Papers, Series 1, Box 2, Folder 74, Auburn University Special Collections & Archives Department.

155. Report of Lieutenant Colonel W.H.A. Speer, Lane Papers; Dedmondt, *Flags of Civil War North Carolina*, 124.

156. Gracey, *Annals of the Sixth Pennsylvania Cavalry*, 273; A.E. Shore, Emory University.

157. *Baltimore Clipper*, August 4, 1864; Caldwell, *History of a Brigade of South Carolinians*, 171; Foster, *Reminiscences and Record of the 6th New York*, 90.

158. Report of Lieutenant Colonel W.H.A. Speer, Lane Papers; Caldwell, *History of a Brigade of South Carolinians*, 171; Conner, *Letters of General James Conner*, 162–63.

159. Report of Lieutenant Colonel John W. McGill, July 29, 1864, James H. Lane Papers, Series 1, Box 2, Folder 74, Auburn University Special Collections & Archives Department.

160. For more on O'Connor, see the original research by Don Caughey at http://regularcavalryincivilwar.wordpress.com/2013/06/26/medal-of-honor-timothy-oconnor-1st-u-s-cavalry.

161. Callais, Lane Papers; A.E. Shore, Emory University.

162. *OR*, vol. 40, pt. 1, 615; Pyne, *History of the First New Jersey Cavalry (Sixteenth Regiment, New Jersey Volunteers)*, 350.

163. *Baltimore Clipper*, August 4, 1864, 1; *OR*, vol. 40, pt. 1, 613, 619.

164. Lieutenant Neil A. Bushnell Memoirs, Mss. 2152, Box 17, vol. 1, the Western Reserve Historical Society.

165. Lieutenant James "Newt" Martin to Sister, August 3, 1864, Martin Letter Collection, South Carolina Relic Room and Military Museum; G.W. Bussey, "Memoirs of Rev. G.W. Bussey," *Recollections and Reminiscences 1861–65*, 412–13; *OR*, vol. 40, pt. 1, 619; Bushnell Memoirs, 413; *OR*, vol. 40, pt. 1, 615.

166. Bushnell Memoirs, 413; *OR*, vol. 40, pt. 1, 652–53.

167. *OR*, vol. 40, pt. 1, 616; S.T. Buikley, *New York Herald*, July 31, 1864.

168. Landrum, *History of Spartanburg County*, 285; Clemmer, *Valor in Gray*, 296–97; Buikley, *New York Herald*; Compiled Service Record of Adam Ballenger, NARA, RG 109.

169. *OR*, vol. 40, pt. 1, 616.

170. Bussey, "Memoirs"; quoted in Wyckoff, *History of the Third South Carolina Infantry*, 292–93; Martin to Sister, South Carolina Relic Room and Military Museum.

171. Volger, "Jim Milling and the War," 11.

172. Conner, *Letters of General James Conner*, 162–63; Harris, *Historical Sketches of the Seventh Regiment*, 53; Reports of McGill, Speer and Bost, Lane Papers; quoted in Clary, *History of the 15th South Carolina*, 218; *OR*, vol. 40, pt. 1, 617; Hess, *Into the Crater*, 45.

Chapter 7

173. *OR*, vol. 40, pt. 1, 613.

174. Ibid.

175. Gibbon, *Personal Recollections of the Civil War*, 248–49. This is one of two incidents that will lead to the estrangement of Hancock and Gibbon and lead to Gibbon's request for a transfer later that year.

176. *OR*, vol. 40, pt. 3, 561.

177. Ibid., vol. 40, pt. 3, 570.

178. Ibid., vol. 40, pt. 1, 426; *OR*, vol. 40, pt. 3, 586.

179. *OR*, vol. 40, pt. 3, 570; *ORN*, series I, vol. 10, 319.

180. *OR*, vol. 40, pt. 3, 587–88; *OR*, vol. 40, pt. 1, 693; Beecher, *History of the First Light Battery*, 526.

181. *New York Herald*, July 31, 1864; Freeman, *R.E. Lee*, 466–67; *OR*, vol. 40, pt. 3, 813.

182. *OR Supplement*, pt. 1, vol. 7, 253.

183. Waring, "Diary of William G. Hinson," 21.

184. *OR*, vol. 40, pt. 3, 561–63.

185. Ibid., vol. 40, pt. 1, 323; *OR*, vol. 40, pt. 3, 563.

186. Lowe, *Meade's Army*, 239; *OR*, vol. 40, pt. 1, 323.

187. Lowe, *Meade's Army*, 239.

188. *OR*, vol. 40, pt. 1, 389; Houghton, *Campaigns of the Seventeenth Maine*, 216–17; Silliker, *Rebel Yell & the Yankee Hurrah*, 185; *OR*, vol. 40, pt. 3, 589.

189. *OR*, vol. 40, pt. 3, 551.

190. *OR Supplement*, vol. 7, 333.

191. Lee, *Memoirs of William Nelson Pendleton*, 355–56.

192. Gallagher, *Fighting for the Confederacy*, 452, 454.

Chapter 8

193. *OR*, vol. 43, pt. 1, 471.

194. Gracey, *Annals of the Sixth Pennsylvania Cavalry*, 273; Cheney, *History of the Ninth Regiment*, 201–2; Lloyd, *History of the First Reg't*, 109.

195. Pfanz, *Letters of General Richard S. Ewell*, 292.

196. Feis, *Grant's Secret Service*, 256; *OR*, vol. 40, pt. 3, 591.

197. *OR*, vol. 40, pt. 3, 598; Walker, *General Hancock*, 250.

198. *OR Supplement*, pt. 1, vol. 7, 252–53.

199. Ibid.

200. Harris, *Historical Sketch of the Seventh Regiment*, 53–54; Speer, *Voices from Cemetery Hill*, 145; W.A. Curtis, "Reminiscences of the War," Duke University.

201. *OR*, vol. 40, pt. 3, 598.

202. Krick, *Civil War Weather in Virginia*, 134.

203. *OR*, vol. 40, pt. 1, 204, 218, 618–20; Beale, *History of the Ninth Virginia Cavalry*, 137; Robert K. Krick, *9ᵗʰ Virginia Cavalry*, 39.

204. Miller, *Harvard's Civil War*, 398; *Richmond Daily Dispatch*, July 30, 1864.

205. *OR*, vol. 40, pt. 1, 766.

206. *OR Supplement*, pt. 1, vol. 7, 345.

207. Gibbon, *Personal Recollections of the Civil War*, 250–51.

208. *OR*, vol. 40, pt. 3, 602–3.

209. Ibid., vol. 40, pt. 3, 601.

210. David Coon Letters; Dyer, *Journal of a Civil War Surgeon*, 183.

Chapter 9

211. Dyer, *Journal of a Civil War Surgeon*, 183; Barnard, *Campaigning with the Irish Brigade*, 122.

212. Silliker, *Rebel Yell & Yankee Hurrah*, 187; Kohl, *Memoirs of Chaplain Life*, 253.

213. *OR*, vol. 40, pt. 3, 646; quoted in Kreiser, *Defeating Lee*, 206.

214. John D. Timmerman, "Pocket Diary, 1864," John D. Timmerman Papers, U.S. Army Heritage and Education Center; Daniel A. Britton to Wife, August 2, 1864. Britton's letters can be found at http://brittoncivilwarletters.blogspot.com.

215. *OR Supplement*, pt. 1, vol. 7, 345, 252–53.

216. Jones, *Rebel War Clerk's Diary*, 258.

217. Long, *Personal Memoirs of U.S. Grant*, 465.

218. Sheridan, *Personal Memoirs*, 451.

219. Pfanz, *Letters of General Richard S. Ewell*, 291.

220. Suderow, "Glory Denied," 31.

221. Gallagher, *Fighting for the Confederacy*, 454; Civil War Trust, "Battle of First Deep Bottom," http://www.civilwar.org/battlefields/first-deep-bottom/first-deep-bottom-history-articles/firstdeepbottomsommers.html.

BIBLIOGRAPHY

NEWSPAPERS

Baltimore Clipper.
Daily Richmond Examiner.
National Tribune.
New York Herald.
New York Times.
New York Tribune.
Richmond Daily Dispatch.
Sunny South.

MANUSCRIPT COLLECTIONS

Augustin E. Shore Correspondence, Manuscript, Archives and Rare Book Library, Emory University.

Benjamin Grubb Humphreys Papers, Mississippi Department of Archives and History.

Civil War Miscellaneous Collection, U.S. Army Heritage and Education Center.

David S. Coon Letters, Library of Congress, Manuscript Division.

James H. Lane Papers, Auburn University Special Collections and Archives Department.

John D. Timmerman Papers, U.S. Army Heritage and Education Center.

Martin Letter Collection, South Carolina Confederate Relic Room and Military Museum.

National Archives, Record Groups 94 and 109.

Parsons Family Papers, Milne Special Collections and Archives, University of New Hampshire.

Schoff Civil War Collection, Clements Library, University of Michigan.

South Caroliniana Library, University South Caroliniana Society Manuscripts Collections, University of South Carolina.

The Western Reserve Historical Society.

PUBLISHED PRIMARY SOURCES

Articles

Sword, Wiley. "Lieut. Frank M. Kelley...Gives Vivid Detail of Grant's Hurried Trip to Deep Bottom." *Blue & Gray* 30, no. 5 (n.d.): 42–44.

Volger, Penny, ed. "Jim Milling and the War, 1862–1865." *Confederate Veteran* 6 (1997).

Waring, Joseph, ed. "The Diary of William G. Hinson During the War of Secession." *South Carolina Historical Magazine* 75 (1974): 14–23 and 111–20.

White, William S. "A Diary of the War or What I Saw of It." *Contributions to a History of the Richmond Howitzer Battalion*. Pamphlet No. 2. Richmond, VA: Carlton McCarthy and Company, 1883.

Books

Agassiz, George R., ed. *Meade's Headquarters, 1863–1865: Letters of Colonel Theodore Lyman from the Wilderness to Appomattox.* Boston: Atlantic Monthly Press, 1922.

Barnard, Sandy, ed. *Campaigning with the Irish Brigade: Pvt. John Ryan, 28th Massachusetts.* Terre Haute, IN: AST Press, 2001.

Basler, Roy, ed. *The Collected Works of Abraham Lincoln.* Vol. 7. New Brunswick, NJ: Rutgers University Press, 1953.

Caldwell, J.F.J. *The History of a Brigade of South Carolinians, Known First as "Gregg's" and Subsequently as "McGowan's Brigade."* Philadelphia: King and Baird Printers, 1866.

Conner, James. *The Letters of General James Conner, C.S.A.* Columbia, SC: State Company, 1933.

Crosland, Charles. *Reminiscences of the Sixties.* Columbia, SC: State Company, 1910.

De Trobriand, Regis. *Four Years with the Army of the Potomac.* Translated by George K. Dauchy. Boston: Ticknor and Company, 1889.

Dowdey, Clifford, and Louis H. Manarin, eds. *The Wartime Papers of Robert E. Lee.* New York: Bramhall House, 1961.

Dyer, J. Franklin. *The Journal of a Civil War Surgeon.* Edited by Michael B. Chesson. Lincoln: University of Nebraska Press, 2003.

Early, Jubal A. *The Campaigns of Gen. Robert E. Lee: An Address by Lieut. General Jubal A. Early, before Washington and Lee University, January 19th, 1872.* Baltimore, MD: John Murphy, 1872.

Fox, William F. *Regimental Losses in the American Civil War, 1861–1865: A Treatise on the Extent and Nature of the Mortuary Losses in the Union Regiments, with Full and Exhaustive Statistics Compiled from the Official Records on File in the State Military Bureaus and at Washington.* Albany, NY: Albany Publishing Company, 1889.

Gallagher, Gary W., ed. *Fighting for the Confederacy: The Personal Recollections of General Edward Porter Alexander*. Chapel Hill: University of North Carolina Press, 1989.

Gibbon, John. *Personal Recollections of the Civil War*. New York: G.P. Putnam's Sons, 1928.

Hagemann, Edward R., ed. *Fighting Rebels and Redskins: Experiences in Army Life of Colonel George B. Sanford, 1861–1892*. Norman: University of Oklahoma Press, 1969.

Jones, John B. *A Rebel War Clerk's Diary*. Vol. 2. Philadelphia: J.B. Lippincott and Company, 1866.

Jones, Terry L., ed. *Campbell Brown's Civil War: With Ewell and the Army of Northern Virginia*. Baton Rouge: Louisiana State University Press, 2001.

Kohl, Lawrence Frederick, ed. *Memoirs of Chaplain Life: Three Years with the Irish Brigade in the Army of the Potomac*. New York: Fordham University Press, 1992.

Lake, Doris, and Wayne L. Cooper, eds. *I Take My Pen in Hand: The Civil War Letters of Two Soldiers and Friends, Sidney A. Lake and Conrad Litt, 100ᵗʰ NY Volunteers, Co. "C,"Buffalo N.Y.* Bloomington, IN: AuthorHouse, 2008.

Lee, Susan P., ed. *Memoirs of William Nelson Pendleton, D.D.: Rector of Latimer Parrish, Lexington, Virginia; Brigadier-General, C.S.A.; Chief of Artillery, Army of Northern Virginia*. Philadelphia: J.D. Lippincott Company, 1893.

Long, E.B., ed. *Personal Memoirs of U.S. Grant*. Cambridge, MA: Da Capo, 2001.

Lowe, David W., ed. *Meade's Army: The Private Notebooks of Lt. Col. Theodore Lyman*. Kent, OH: Kent State University Press, 2007.

Mackey, Thomas C., ed. *A Documentary History of the Civil War Era*. Vol. 2, *Political Arguments*. Knoxville: University of Tennessee Press, 2013.

Military Order of the Loyal Legion of the United States. In Memoriam. Major General Winfield Scott Hancock, United States Army. Philadelphia, 1886.

Nicolay, John George, and John Hay, eds. *Abraham Lincoln: Complete Works, Comprising His Speeches, State Papers, and Miscellaneous Writings.* Vol. 2. New York: Century Company, 1920.

Official Records of the Union and Confederate Navies in the War of the Rebellion. Series I, vol. 10. Washington, D.C.: Government Printing Office, 1900.

Papers of the Military Historical Society of Massachusetts. Vol. 4, *The Wilderness Campaign, May–June 1864.* Boston: Military Historical Society of Massachusetts, 1905.

Pfanz, Donald C., ed. *The Letters of General Richard S. Ewell: Stonewall's Successor.* Knoxville: University of Tennessee Press, 2012.

Porter, Horace. *Campaigning with Grant.* New York: Century Company, 1906.

Recollections and Reminiscences 1861–1865 through World War I. Vol. 1. South Carolina United Daughters of the Confederacy, 1990.

Rodenbough, Theophilus F., ed. *From Everglade to Canon with the Second Dragoons.* New York: D. Van Nostrand, 1875.

Samito, Christian G., ed. *"Fear Was Not in Him": The Civil War Letters of Francis C. Barlow, U.S.A.* New York: Fordham University Press, 2004.

Sheridan, Philip H. *Personal Memoirs of P.H. Sheridan.* Vol. 1. New York: Charles L. Webster and Company, 1888.

Silliker, Ruth L., ed. *The Rebel Yell & the Yankee Hurrah: The Civil War Journal of a Maine Volunteer, Private John W. Haley, 17th Maine Regiment.* Camden, NJ: Down East Books, 1985.

Simon, John Y., ed. *Papers of Ulysses S. Grant.* Vol. 11, *June 1–August 15, 1864.* Carbondale: Southern Illinois University Press, 1967.

Speer, Allen Paul, ed. *Voices from Cemetery Hill: The Civil War Diary, Reports, and Letters of Colonel William Henry Asbury Speer, 1861–1864.* Johnson City, TN: Overmountain Press, 1997.

Styple, William B., ed. *Generals in Bronze: Interviewing the Commanders of the Civil War*. Kearny: Belle Grove Publishing Company, 2005.

Sumner, Merlin E., ed. *The Diary of Cyrus Comstock*. Dayton, OH: Morningside Press, 1987.

Supplement to the Official Records of the Union and Confederate Armies. Part I, vol. 7. Wilmington, NC: Broadfoot Publishing Company, 1997.

Taylor, Gary Nelson, ed. *Saddle and Saber: Civil War Letters of Corporal Nelson Taylor, Ninth New York State Volunteer Cavalry to His Father Shubael Taylor and Sister Hannah, Clifton Park, New York, November 14, 1861–October 30, 1864*. Bowie, MD: Heritage Books, 1993.

The War of the Rebellion: A Compilation of the Official Records of the Union and Confederate Armies. Series I, vol. 40, parts 1–3. Washington, D.C.: United States Government Printing Office, 1889.

Weld, Stephen Minot. *War Diary and Letters of Stephen Minot Weld*. Boston: Massachusetts Historical Society, 1979.

West, Robert Jerald L., ed. *Found Among the Privates: Recollections of Holcomb's Legion 1861–1864, by James L. Strain and Adolphus E. Fant, Correspondents to the* Union County News, *Union County, S.C.* Sharon, SC: privately published, 1997.

White, Russell C., ed. *The Civil War Diary of Wyman S. White: First Sergeant of Company F, 2nd United States Sharpshooter Regiment, 1861–1865*. Baltimore, MD: Butternut and Blue, 1991.

Wixson, Neal E., ed. *Echoes from the Boys of Company "H."* Bloomington, IN: iUniverse, 2008.

SECONDARY SOURCES

Articles

Suderow, Bryce A. "Glory Denied: The First Battle of Deep Bottom, July 27th–29th, 1864." *North & South* 3, no. 7 (September 2000): 17–32.

————. "War Along the James." *North & South* 6, no. 3 (April 2003): 12–23.

Ware, John N. "Enroughty, Darby and General McClellan." In *American Heritage* 7, no. 2 (February 1956).

Books

Beale, R.L.T. *History of the Ninth Virginia Cavalry in the War Between the States.* Richmond, VA: B.F. Johnson Publishing Company, 1899.

Beecher, Herbert W. *History of the First Light Battery, Connecticut Volunteers, 1861–1865; Personal Records and Reminiscences; The Story of the Battery from Its Organization to the Present Time; Compiled from Official Records, Personal Interviews, Private Diaries, War Histories, and Individual Experiences.* New York: A.T. DeLaMare Printing and Publishing Company, 1901.

Billings, John D. *The History of the Tenth Massachusetts Battery of Light Artillery in the War of the Rebellion, 1862–1865.* Boston: Arakelyan Press, 1909.

Cavanaugh, Michael A., and William Marvel. *The Battle of the Crater: "The Horrid Pit," June 25–August 6, 1864.* Lynchburg, VA: H.E. Howard Inc., 1989.

Cheney, Newell. *History of the Ninth Regiment New York Volunteer Cavalry: War of 1861 to 1865.* New York: Martin Merz and Son, 1901.

Clary, James B. *A History of the 15th South Carolina Volunteer Infantry Regiment, 1861–1865.* Wilmington, NC: Broadfoot Publishing Company, 2007.

Clemmer, Gregg S. *Valor in Gray: The Recipients of the Confederate Medal of Honor.* Staunton, VA: Hearthside Publishing Company, 1998.

Davis, William C., and James I. Robertson Jr., eds. *Virginia at War, 1864.* Lexington: University of Kentucky Press, 2009.

Davis, William C., ed. *The Confederate General.* Vol. 3. N.p.: National Historical Society, 1991.

Dedmondt, Glenn. *The Flags of Civil War North Carolina*. Gretna, LA: Pelican Publishing Company, 2003.

Dickey, Luther S. *History of the Eighty-fifth Pennsylvania Volunteer Infantry 1861–1865, Comprising an Authentic Narrative of Casey's Division at the Battle of Seven Pines*. New York: J.C. and W.E. Powers, 1915.

Driver, Robert J. *The 1ˢᵗ and 2ⁿᵈ Rockbridge Artillery*. Lynchburg, VA: H.E. Howard Inc., 1987.

Dufour, Charles L. *Nine Men in Gray*. Lincoln: University of Nebraska Press, 1963.

Feis, William B. *Grant's Secret Service: The Intelligence War from Belmont to Appomattox*. Lincoln: University of Nebraska Press, 2002.

Foster, Alonzo. *Reminiscences and Record of the 6ᵗʰ New York V.V. Cavalry*. Brooklyn, NY: Alonzo Foster, 1892.

Freeman, Douglas Southall. *R.E. Lee: A Biography*. Vol. 3. New York: Charles Scribner's Sons, 1935.

Gallagher, Gary W. *The Confederate War: How Popular Will, Nationalism, and Military Strategy Could Not Stave Off Defeat*. Cambridge, MA: Harvard University Press, 1997.

Gracey, S.L. *Annals of the Sixth Pennsylvania Cavalry*. Philadelphia: E.H. Butler and Company, 1868.

Green, Bennett Wood. *Word Book of Virginia Folk Speech*. Richmond, VA: Wm. Ellis Jones, Book and Job Printer, 1890.

Harris, James. *Historical Sketches of the Seventh Regiment North Carolina*. Mooresville, NC: Mooresville Printing Company, 1893.

Hess, Earl J. *Into the Crater: The Mine Attack at Petersburg*. Columbia: University of South Carolina Press, 2010.

Holland, Darryl. *24ᵗʰ Virginia Cavalry*. Lynchburg, VA: H.E. Howard Inc., 1997.

Houghton, Edwin B. *The Campaigns of the Seventeenth Maine*. Portland, ME: Short and Loring, 1866.

Kreiser, Lawrence A. *Defeating Lee: A History of the Second Corps, Army of the Potomac*. Bloomington: Indiana University, 2011.

Krick, Robert K. *Civil War Weather in Virginia*. Tuscaloosa: University of Alabama Press, 2007.

———. *9th Virginia Cavalry*. Lynchburg, VA: H.E. Howard, Inc., 1982.

Landrum, J.B.O. *History of Spartanburg County: Embracing an Account of Many Important Events, and Biographical Sketches of Statesmen, Divines, and Other Public Men, and the Names of Many Others Worthy of Record in the History of their County*. Atlanta, GA: Franklin Printing and Publishing Company, 1900.

Lloyd, William P. *History of the First Reg't Pennsylvania Reserve Cavalry: From Its Organization, August, 1861, to September, 1864, with a List of Names of All Officers and Enlisted Men Who Have Ever Belonged to the Regiment*. Philadelphia: King and Baird, 1864.

Maxfield, Albert, and Robert Brady Jr. *Company D, Eleventh Maine Infantry Volunteers in the War of the Rebellion*. New York: Press of Thos. Humphrey, 1890.

Miller, Richard F. *Harvard's Civil War: A History of the Twentieth Massachusetts Volunteer Infantry*. Lebanon, NH: University Press of New England, 2005.

Naval History Division. *Civil War Navy Chronology, 1861–1865*. Washington, D.C.: Department of the Navy, 1971.

Nevins, Allan. *The War for the Union*. Vol. 4, *The Organized War to Victory, 1864–1865*. New York: Charles Scribner's Sons, 1971.

Pfanz, Donald C. *Richard S. Ewell: A Soldier's Life*. Chapel Hill: University of North Carolina Press, 1998.

Power, J. Tracy *Lee's Miserables: Life in the Army of Northern Virginia from the Wilderness to Appomattox*. Chapel Hill: University of North Carolina Press, 1998.

Pyne, Henry R. *The History of the First New Jersey Cavalry (Sixteenth Regiment, New Jersey Volunteers)*. Trenton, NJ: J.A. Beecher, 1871.

Rawlinson, Mary Stewart, ed. *The Walter Stewart Family History*. Columbia, SC: State Printing Company, 1982.

Rhodes, John H. *The History of Battery B, First Regiment Rhode Island Light Artillery in the War to Preserve the Union 1861–1865*. Providence, RI: Snow and Farham, 1894.

Roe, Alfred S., Charles B. Amory, John C. Cook and George Hill. *The Twenty-fourth Regiment Massachusetts Volunteers, 1861–1866, "New England Guard Regiment."* Worcester, MA: Twenty-fourth Veteran Association, 1907.

Sheehan-Dean, Aaron. *Why Confederates Fought: Family and Nation in Civil War Virginia*. Chapel Hill: University of North Carolina Press, 2007.

Stevens, Charles A. *Berdan's United States Sharpshooters in the Army of the Potomac, 1861–1865*. St. Paul, MN: C.A. Stevens, 1892.

The Story of One Regiment: The Eleventh Maine Infantry Volunteers in the War of the Rebellion. New York: Press of J.J. Little and Company, 1896.

Stowits, George H. *History of the One Hundredth Regiment of New York State Volunteers*. Buffalo, NY: House of Matthews and Warren, 1870.

Sturkey, O. Lee. *Hampton Legion Infantry C.S.A.* Wilmington, NC: Broadfoot Publishing Company, 2008.

Trumbull, H. Clay. *The Knightly Soldier: A Biography of Major Henry Ward Camp, 10th Conn Volunteers*. Boston: Nichols and Noyes, 1865.

Walker, Cornelius Irvine. *The Life of Lieutenant General Richard Heron Anderson of the Confederate States Army*. Charleston, SC: Art Publishing Company, 1917.

Walker, Francis A. *General Hancock*. New York: D. Appleton and Company, 1894.

———. *History of the Second Army Corps in the Army of the Potomac*. New York: Charles Scribner's Sons, 1886.

Warner, Ezra J. *Generals in Blue: Lives of the Union Commanders.* Baton Rouge: Louisiana State University Press, 1964.

————. *Generals in Gray: Lives of the Confederate Commanders.* Baton Rouge: Louisiana State University Press, 1959.

Wyckoff, Mac. *A History of the Third South Carolina Infantry, 1861–1865.* Wilmington, NC: Broadfoot Publishing Company, 2008.

Young, Alfred C. *Lee's Army during the Overland Campaign: A Numerical Study.* Baton Rouge: Louisiana State University Press, 2013.

Index

About the Author

James S. Price is the Historic Site Manager for Bristoe Station Battlefield Heritage Park in Prince William County. He received his MA in military history from Norwich University in 2009. His first book, *The Battle of New Market Heights: Freedom Will Be Theirs by the Sword*, was nominated in the nonfiction category for the fifteenth annual Library of Virginia Literary Awards. The *Journal of Southern History* noted that "this slim volume offers considerable insight regarding the black military experience." He contributed the essay "Storming the Heights of the Meuse: The 29th and 33rd Divisions Fight for Control of the High Ground, 8–16 October" in Edward G. Lengel's volume *A Companion to the Meuse-Argonne Campaign*, published in 2014. James also writes about different aspects of Civil War history on his award-winning blog, "Freedom by the Sword: A Historian's Journey through the American Civil War Era."

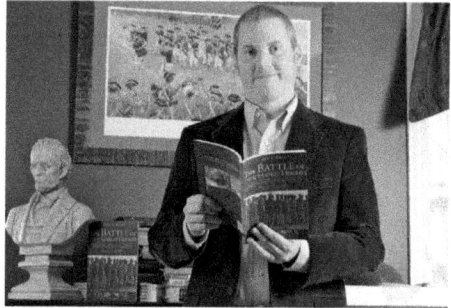

From the Free Lance-Star.

www.ingramcontent.com/pod-product-compliance
Lightning Source LLC
Chambersburg PA
CBHW060804100426
42813CB00004B/943